Lighthouses
OF New England

Your Guide to the Lighthouses
of Maine, New Hampshire, Vermont,
Massachusetts, Rhode Island,
and Connecticut

Text by Jon Marcus
Photography by Susan Cole Kelly

A Pictorial
Discovery Guide

VOYAGEUR PRESS

Edited by Gretchen Bratvold
Designed by Maria Friedrich
Printed in Hong Kong

First hardcover edition
01   02   03   04   05   5   4   3   2   1

First softcover edition
02   03   04   05   06   5   4   3   2   1

Library of Congress Cataloging-in-Publication Data
Marcus, Jon, 1960–
     Lighthouses of New England : your guide to
the lighthouses of Maine, New Hampshire,
Vermont, Massachusetts, Rhode Island, and
Connecticut / text by Jon Marcus ; photography
by Susan Cole Kelly.
          p. cm. — (Pictorial discovery guide)
     Includes bibliographical references and index.
     ISBN 0-89658-484-4
     ISBN 0-89658-617-0 (pbk.)
     1. Lighthouses—New England—Pictorial works.
I.Title. II. Series.

     VK1024.N38 M37 2001
     387.1'55'0974—dc21   00-043794

Distributed in Canada by Raincoast Books
9050 Shaughnessy Street, Vancouver, B.C. V6P 6E5

Published by Voyageur Press, Inc.
123 North Second Street, P.O. Box 338
Stillwater, MN 55082 U.S.A.
651-430-2210, fax 651-430-2211
books@voyageurpress.com
www.voyageurpress.com

Page 1: The lighthouse at Pemaquid Point, Maine, has marked the entrance to Muscongus Bay since 1835.

Pages 2–3: Owl's Head Light, built in 1826, marks the entrance to Maine's Rockland Harbor.

Page 3 inset: The keepers at Highland (Cape Cod) Light had to climb sixty-nine winding steps to the lantern room, 183 feet above the sea. The 404-ton lighthouse was moved 450 feet away from the eroding shore in 1996.

Facing page: Proceeds from this special license plate depicting Nauset Light on Cape Cod support economic development and tourism promotion on the Cape and nearby Martha's Vineyard and Nantucket. (Courtesy of the Massachusetts Registry of Motor Vehicles)

Page 6: Sunrise plays against Bass Harbor Head Light above the rocky coast of Maine's Mount Desert Island.

Page 7 inset: Automated in 1952, Long Point Light in Provincetown on Cape Cod is home now only to seagulls.

Dedication

To my grandmothers, Alice Cole and Mary Kelly. Alice lived a privileged young life within sight of the lights at New Bedford, Massachusetts, and Mary passed by them on her voyage to America. Both women later raised families alone and did what had to be done in hard times. — Susan Cole Kelly

Photographic Notes

Photos for this book were made over a period of several years. Film ranged from Fuji Velvia to Kodak Elite to Kodak E100VS, chosen for its beautiful color saturation and extreme sharpness. Kelly used the Canon EOS system of cameras, most recently the EOS-3. Lenses included the Canon EF 28–105mm and the Canon EF 75–300mm Image Stabilizer. The Canon TS-E 24mm Tilt and Shift lens was used to reduce the perspective distortion of wide-angle architectural images. Most of the photographs were made with the camera on a tripod, either the lightweight Benbo Trekker or the sturdy Uni-Lock. A backpack-style camera bag was used, to enable the photographer to climb on rocky cliffs with hands free.

Contents

First Lights

Steadfast, serene, immovable, the same
Year after year, through all the silent night
Burns on forevermore that quenchless flame,
Shines on that inextinguishable light!

"The Lighthouse" by Henry Wadsworth Longfellow

New England's rocky shore is as perilous as it is picturesque. From the gentle dunes of Cape Cod to the piney forests of Maine, it beckons sirenlike to mariners across the interceding shoals.

It was, of course, inevitable that North America's first lighthouses would rise above this craggy coast—not only the first to be built, but also the first lights of the New World to be seen by ships arriving from the Old. Here made port the nation's early seaborne commerce, its fishing fleet and whaling vessels, and the merchant vessels of the profitable China trade. Here the natural sea-lanes of the Labrador Current and the Gulf Stream hug the shore so tightly that they leave behind a detritus of wrecked ships. Here thick banks of fog, winter storms, surf, and cold still claim the hardy souls that make their livings from the sea.

The early colonists used bonfires or burning barrels of pitch to warn their ships away from shore. It was a logical next step to raise the lights to towers where they could be seen from farther out to sea. Behind the thick glass the lamps were lit with whale oil, kerosene, or even lard, and turned with weights. This turned out to be so effective a means of communication that Paul Revere and friends would emulate it when they arranged to have a lantern in the steeple of the Old North Church to warn waiting riders in the distance that the British had begun to march toward Lexington and Concord on the eve of the Revolution.

Just a beacon's length from the Old North Church, the first true lighthouse in North America was built: Boston Light on Boston Harbor's Little Brewster Island,

lit for the first time in September 1716. The colonies' first fog signal was a cannon that was fired from the island in answer to a ship's call. Boston Light would literally witness history: Its keepers watched the 1813 battle between the U.S. ship *Chesapeake* and the British vessel *Shannon* in the War of 1812, when Captain James Lawrence of the *Chesapeake* is said to have muttered the immortal words "Don't give up the ship!" as he lay mortally wounded on the bloody deck.

Stories like these have captured the American imagination, and with it the attention of poets, novelists, and artists. Lighthouses are romantic and nostalgic, and the same dramatic coast the lights were built to guard provides extraordinary settings for them. Bass Harbor Head Light on Mount Desert Island in Maine has as its backdrop the breathtaking Acadia National Park, for instance. Nauset Light, built in 1838 on Cape Cod, was immortalized in a painting by artist Edward Hopper. Lighthouses are associated with heroic rescues, tragic deaths, ghosts, pirates, isolation, and privation, located as they often are on islands, desolate peninsulas, and cliffs. Lovers have been found locked in last embraces on wrecked ships near beacon towers that could not protect them from the winds or the currents. Rumrunners and gangsters have used the offshore lights as hideouts.

Four of the first five U.S. lighthouses were in Massachusetts and Rhode Island (the fifth was in New Orleans). Massachusetts claims not only the oldest and last staffed lighthouse, but also the oldest wooden lighthouse, Plymouth (Gurnet) Light in Plymouth Harbor—the only lighthouse known to have been struck by a cannonball,

The waning sun falls against Maine's Fort Point Light, which stands above the west side of the Penobscot River.

thanks to a panicked gunner on a grounded British frigate during the Revolutionary War.

The new nation took up the issue of reliable lighthouses as one of its first items of business. The ninth law enacted by the first Congress put twelve existing colonial lighthouses under federal control and created the Lighthouse Establishment as part of the Treasury Department (it shifted to what was then jointly known as the Commerce and Labor Department in 1903, and to the Coast Guard in 1939). In 1789, George Washington himself, accompanied by the Marquis de Lafayette, visited Portsmouth Harbor Light, one of those original twelve lighthouses. Another, Portland Head Light in Maine, was finished in 1790 and has been lit without interruption since. The first lighthouse built entirely by the federal government, New York's Montauk Point Light, completed in 1797, was the first landmark to greet arriving immigrants, becoming as much a symbol of America as the Statue of Liberty.

Lighthouses have been built of virtually every material considered strong enough to weather the New England winter, but predominantly of indestructible New England granite. In 1844, the first cast-iron lighthouse was built on Long Island Head in Boston, replacing the deteriorating rubblestone-and-granite tower that had stood on that site since 1820. One of the greatest innovations in lighthouse construction was the cast-iron lighthouse drilled into rock at Minot's Ledge Light near Cohasset, Massachusetts, where there had been forty wrecks in one ten-year period beginning in the 1830s. Yet the lighthouse itself would be swept away by the fury of the sea. Gay Head Light on Martha's Vineyard is made of brick. So is the Victorian red brick lighthouse on the 160-foot-tall cliffs of Block Island's Monhegan Bluffs. Though this structure weighs 2,000 tons, preservationists succeeded in moving it 300 feet from the eroding shore in 1993.

It is their keepers who breathed life into the lights, showing faithfulness and courage despite low pay and harsh conditions. They would struggle to fill the time, even growing roses in the salty soil. In the 1920s, William Wincapaw, of Friendship, Maine, started the tradition of the Flying Santa, bringing holiday gifts to the lonely keepers and their families.

Gay Head Light warns mariners around the fog-bound cliffs of Martha's Vineyard and marks a ledge that sailors call the Devil's Bridge.

Marking the entrance to Nantucket Harbor, Brant Point Light is America's second-oldest light station.

Many of the bravest lighthouse keepers were women, who were among the first female federal employees; most inherited the job from husbands or fathers who had died. There were 138 women employed as keepers between 1828 and 1947. Abbie Burgess got her first trial as a keeper when she was seventeen. Trapped for a month in stormy weather at the Matinicus Rock Light in Maine when her father went ashore to get provisions, she stayed in the tower, keeping the light lit. Her gravestone is a replica of the lighthouse. Ida Lewis, the keeper of Lime Rock Light in Newport, Rhode Island, took over the job from her father when he became ill. Among other chores, she rowed her younger siblings back and forth to school each day. Lewis is credited with saving dozens of seafarers and received a congratulatory visit from President Ulysses S. Grant. When she died, boat bells in Newport Harbor tolled all night.

Even with so many stories, a few New England lights enjoy particular distinction. For example, stubby Brant Point Light at the entrance to Nantucket Harbor, built in 1746 and the second oldest lighthouse in the coun-

try, is decorated with a giant wreath to welcome visitors at Christmas. It has had to be rebuilt seven times. Highland (Cape Cod) Light, built in 1797 and moved away from the eroding shore in 1996, can be seen from twenty-three miles out to sea, where it is the welcome first sight of land for many sailors. West Quoddy Head Light in Maine, built in 1808, clings to the easternmost point of land in the United States. Its beacon sweeps the banks of fog that roll in from the Bay of Fundy. Point Judith Light, built in 1810 in Rhode Island, guards one of the most dangerous stretches of American coastline, called the Graveyard of the Atlantic. The Isles of Shoals (White Island) Light in New Hampshire, built in 1821 as just a tower with a lantern, straddles an island chain settled in 1614. Captain Kidd is said to have buried some of his treasure here.

Even in this day of satellite navigation, mariners still rely heavily on lighthouses, not for their history or architecture, but for their life-saving beacons. A photograph of Maine's Cape Neddick ("the Nubble") Light was even launched aboard the *Voyager* spacecraft in 1977 as one

Hendricks Head Light in West Southport, Maine, was built in 1875 at the mouth of the Sheepscot River to replace a simple lantern room atop a keeper's house.

of several prominent landmarks meant to help identify Earth. Though most lighthouses now are automated, some still serve as housing for U.S. Coast Guardsmen and others. Yet as they have been automated, many lighthouses have been allowed to deteriorate. Municipal governments, private owners, state parks, and friends organizations are trying to preserve them with the help of new laws that allow their transfer to private ownership. Their success will help ensure Longfellow's promise that America's first lights "burn on forevermore."

The sturdy granite lighthouse at the north end of Block Island in Rhode Island is affectionately called "Old Granitesides."

CHAPTER 1

Legacy of the Lights:

The Story of the Lighthouse Service

Left: *An archetypal cast-iron-style New England lighthouse, Nobska Point Light guides mariners to Woods Hole on Cape Cod. A lighthouse has stood on this spot since 1829. Today the keeper's quarters serves as housing for the commander of the Woods Hole Coast Guard base.*

Above: *In 1854, Gay Head Light on Martha's Vineyard became one of the first in America to receive a beehive-style first-order Fresnel lens, replacing a crude and feeble magnifying lantern that was so dim it was often impossible to see. The lens is now on display in the Martha's Vineyard Historical Museum.*

As the rising waters nudged his heavy wooden longboat off the rocky banks of Little Brewster Island, George Worthylake reflected that the tide of his misfortune also finally seemed to be turning.

It was November 3, 1718, a little more than two years since Worthylake had first agreed to take the job of keeper of the lonely lighthouse tower on the island in the heart of Boston Harbor. That decision almost instantly began to seem like a mistake. No one really knew what the position would entail, since Boston Light was the first and only lighthouse in the colonies. But Worthylake had let his swagger get the best of him. He was familiar with these waters, having lived on nearby Georges Island. And he figured he could easily augment his annual salary of fifty pounds by raising sheep and working part time as a harbor pilot, steering vessels through the narrow channel, past the rocky shoals and shallow sandbars to the docks.

Worthylake's responsibilities as keeper, however, turned out to be more time-consuming than he had expected. From the time it was first illuminated on September 14, 1716, the light had proven a demanding mistress. Trimming the wicks, hauling the oil, cleaning the glass—his duties left him little time for piloting. He also had to serve as health officer, inspecting each incoming ship for plague or other illness. Worse still, nearly sixty of his sheep had wandered onto Great Brewster Spit during a gale, where they had been stranded and were drowned by the incoming tide as he watched, helpless, from the tower.

But now his bad luck seemed to be lifting like the morning fog. After months of pleading, Worthylake had finally persuaded the town fathers to increase his salary from fifty pounds to seventy; his trip ashore was a happy one to pick up his pay, supplies, and even a few luxuries for his wife and daughter Ruth, who both came with him, along with a slave. Their errands done, they headed back together toward the lighthouse. It was a slow journey in a rowboat, but Worthylake's spirits were high. It seemed another good omen when his little party was invited aboard an anchored sloop along the way. He gratefully accepted.

Invited by a passenger named John Edge, the Worthylakes ate and drank aboard the ship, "though not to excess," as witnesses would later tell it. Still, it was 11 o'clock by the time they left again for the lighthouse, and midnight when they finally approached the island. Relieved to see him, his daughter Ann and a friend who had stayed behind watched as Worthylake maneuvered the overloaded boat toward the rocks of Little Brewster Island.

Their relief quickly turned to horror as they saw it capsize. All aboard were drowned. When the tide went out the next day, the body of George Worthylake, America's first lighthouse keeper, was discovered washed ashore on the same sodden spit where his sheep had been lost. Incredibly, Worthylake's successor, Robert Saunders, also drowned days after taking the job.

Worthylake's fate is the first of many extraordinary tales of U.S. lights, which have become particularly associated with New England and New York as the lonely outposts of their beautiful but deadly coasts. Their history of danger, isolation, and privation has captivated the American imagination—so much so that, even then, a thirteen-year-old apprentice printer named Benjamin Franklin wrote a ballad about the Worthylake catastrophe and peddled copies on the streets of Boston. Adding to the intrigue was a mystery: Worthylake's pay was missing from his pockets when his body was discovered. He is buried in Boston's famous Copp's Hill Burying Ground.

Rising Lights

The construction of Boston Light, and Worthylake's fight over his pay, also marked the beginning of a less well-known saga: the long history of the organization and administration behind U.S. lighthouses, and the people who decided where, when, and how to build and run them.

That story dates as far back as the earliest European exploration. With dense woods and rocky soil at their backs, coastal settlers turned to the sea for food, whale oil, trade, and transportation. But the ragged coast, extreme weather, fog, and shoals took a toll in sunken ships and drowned sailors. The sandy banks of Cape Cod, the rocky coast of Maine, and the tricky channels into colonial ports were particularly risky. As shipping—and shipwrecks—multiplied, so did the influence of shippers. They began to clamor for lights that would be more effective than bonfires set on a high point of land, or kettles of burning tar at the top of a pole.

The colonial merchants of Boston—then North America's most important port—were the first to finally demand action, petitioning the Massachusetts General Court in 1713 for a "lantern on some head land at the entrance of the harbor of Boston for the direction of ships and vessels in the nighttime bound into said harbor." A few rudimentary beacons already existed on the edges of the harbor, one of them since 1673 at Point Allerton in Hull. But the merchants wanted an enclosed light in the center of the harbor, near the shipping channel. Lawmakers set up a committee to consider the idea and approved the building of Boston Light on July 23, 1715. "Whereas the want of a lighthouse at the entrance to the harbor of Boston hath been a great discouragement to navigation by the loss of the lives and estates of several of his majesty's subjects," the legislature decreed, a new light would now be kept aglow "from sun setting to sun rising." North America's premier lighthouse cast its beacon for the first time on September 14, 1716. Its upkeep was to be paid from a tax on shippers of a penny per ton in each direction. Coastal ships were charged two shillings per visit, and fishing vessels five shillings a year.

Other colonial ports would follow this model, with local authorities siting, funding, and controlling their lighthouses. Safety was not always a primary concern. In the case of Boston Light, for instance, a puritanical legislature refused to add a badly needed lightning rod, proclaiming it would be both "vanity and irreligion for the arm of flesh to presume to avert the stroke of heaven." There was almost no coordination between the ports, and lighthouses continued to be built for local needs during the eighteenth century, rather than as part of a system. But compared to the later era of standardization, this period of decentralization was to leave the Northeast with a considerably more interesting variety of lighthouse architecture.

Thirty years passed after the establishment of Boston Light before another lighthouse was built in North America, this time in response to a proposal by sea captains at the January 24, 1746, town meeting on Nantucket Island. Brant Point Light was completed April 28. In 1774, the town began to levy shipping fees to underwrite the lighthouse, but in this case the captains balked. True to that antitaxation era, they appealed to the General Court, but the court sided with the town.

Yankee thrift also held up the third lighthouse, Beavertail Light in Rhode Island. There the cautious legislature collected levies for the lighthouse from Newport shippers for eighteen years before it was finally built in 1749. In Connecticut, a lottery was used to raise money for a lighthouse at New London Harbor built in 1760. The first navigational light in New Hampshire was a lantern hoisted to the top of the flagpole at Fort William and Mary in Portsmouth, paid for by a levy on vessels entering and leaving Portsmouth Harbor. In 1740 Nantucket had first asked for a lighthouse at Great Point, where many whaling ships were being wrecked. It took forty-four years before the General Court agreed to start construction.

By then the Revolutionary War had drained most local treasuries. By 1787, when Massachusetts Governor John Hancock authorized a light at Portland Harbor (still part of Massachusetts at the time), he ordered it to be built of "rubblestone," a cheap construction material consisting of field stones that could be carried to the site by workmen and set in locally quarried lime-

Built in 1826, the original squat Owl's Head Light still stands, marking the Rockland Harbor entrance. Though it was automated in 1989, it still has its 1856 fourth-order Fresnel lens.

America's Front Yard

*B*oston Light may be the nation's quintessential lighthouse, but it doesn't stand alone in Boston Harbor. It is at the center of the watery tableau that is America's front yard, an urban archipelago populated by pirates, ghosts, shipwrecks, buried treasure, secret passageways, forts, and dungeons.

The first Europeans to look out over Boston Harbor came not in tall ships, but in longboats. Vikings under the command of Leif Ericson's brother, Thorwald, are believed to have dropped anchor in the harbor six centuries before the Pilgrims landed, continuing up the Charles River to a settlement they christened Norumbega. The site of the supposed settlement is commemorated by a stone tower, built by Viking enthusiasts in 1897, and the supports of the Longfellow Bridge across the Charles are shaped like the bows of longboats bound upriver.

Europeans settled Boston Harbor's Georges Island in 1618, two years before the Puritans set up their colony in mainland Boston. Later, it became the site of Fort Warren, which took twenty-five years to build, beginning in 1833, and is impeccably preserved. The star-shaped fort surrounds a grassy parade ground and has emplacements for 350 cannon, a semisubterranean prison, underground passageways, a drawbridge, and a shot hoist elevator that could lift 1,000-pound rounds to massive guns installed when ironclad ships came into service.

Fort Warren never fired its guns at an invading ship, although it once almost accidentally hit the Nantasket ferry during target practice. But more than 3,000 Confederates were imprisoned here, including Confederate vice president Alexander Hamilton Stephens. Political prisoners reportedly slept late, ate large lunches, smoked cigars, and took long strolls on the shoreline, while Union officers stationed on the island were credited with composing the ballad "John Brown's Body" in their ample leisure time.

Despite this lax pace, there were several executions at Fort Warren, including that of a prisoner's wife known only as the Woman in Black, who dressed as a man and smuggled herself onto the island in a bid to free her husband. Her last wish was to be hanged in women's clothing—black drapes from the mess hall fashioned into a crude dress. Since then, there have been more than twenty sightings of a ghostlike figure dressed in black; there are even court-martial records of sentries who shot at this apparition in the dark. One winter, a woman's footprints were discovered in the snow coming from and leading nowhere.

The largest harbor island, Peddocks, also has a giant fort, but it's an eerie ruin, abandoned after World War II and overgrown with trees. Built in the 1890s, Fort Andrews housed artillery and, later, antiaircraft guns and observation stations. More than 1,000 Italian prisoners were held there during World War II; many later returned to settle in Boston. Summer residents attended the white wooden church beside the pier, but the cottage community that shared the island with the fort has since been abandoned. One islander working in her garden found what turned out to be the remains of a Native American man who lived 4,100 years ago, the oldest skeleton ever discovered in New England.

The other islands housed reformatories, asylums, poorhouses, hospitals, prisons, barracks, and the homes of the eccentric rich. Atlantic Coast pirates hid out here, and it is on Gallops Island that the notorious Long Ben Avery was said to have buried his treasure. In response, the fearful townspeople left the bodies of captured pirates rotting in chains as warnings at the entrance to the harbor on Bird Island and on tiny Nix's Mate, which has since eroded to no more than a tidal flat marked with a stone. Resort hotels were built on several of the islands, but were shut down for illegal boxing and other, unspecified, vices.

One of the most interesting islands in the harbor is not, technically, an island. Castle Island, which was connected to the mainland in 1891, is the site of the oldest continually used military fortification in the United States—Fort Independence, established in 1634.

Like other harbor islands, Castle Island has a literary history. The friends of a Lieutenant Robert Massie, who was shot dead in 1837 in a Christmas Day duel over a card game, sealed his killer alive in a chamber deep in the dungeons of the fort. A sullen private named Edgar Allen Poe, posted to Fort Independence ten years later, heard about the incident and used it as the basis for his story "The Cask of Amontillado." In 1905, workers repairing an abandoned casement found a skeleton in military uniform sealed in the wall.

Lovells Island, near the middle of the harbor, has a history of shipwrecks. In 1782, the French man-of-war *Magnifique* went aground here, laden with gold coins that were never found, as it sailed into Boston Harbor as part of the great French fleet supporting the Americans in their war against King George III of England. At the time, Boston Light was just a ruin, having been destroyed by the retreating British at the outset of the Revolutionary War; the beacon was not rebuilt until the next year. But the seventy-four-gun warship sank in broad daylight. The incident was blamed on a harbor pilot named David Darling, who had come aboard to guide the ship to shore.

Desperate to prevent a rift with their only major ally, the Americans presented France with the seventy-four-gun USS *America* as compensation for the lost *Magnifique*. But the *America* also had been promised to John Paul Jones, the new nation's greatest naval hero, who angrily resigned his commission. Darling lost his job as harbor pilot but became sexton of the Old North Church, succeeding the man who hung the lanterns to signal that the British were coming.

If there had been any doubt of Boston Harbor's central role in history, it went down with the *Magnifique*.

The original Boston Light was a stone tower built and maintained with a tax on shipping. Blown up by the retreating British during the Revolutionary War, it was rebuilt in 1783.

stone powder. He probably would have preferred it not be built at all, but the owners of seventy-four Portland Harbor ships had been petitioning him since 1784. The work proceeded so slowly that Portland Head Light was not finished until 1791.

That was when the laggard pace of lighting America's shores suddenly started speeding up.

Federal Administration

Exuberant over their success at winning independence from the Mother Country, the former colonists were still a little testy in the late 1780s about how much power ought to be surrendered to their new central government. But the men who had devised the Constitution in the first place reasoned no one would mind if Congress took over the lighthouses. On the contrary; the states would probably be happy to be rid of them. And adding lights would bolster fishing, shipbuilding, and foreign trade, all badly depressed by the war.

Which is how it came to pass that Massachusetts Congressman Elbridge Gerry introduced the ninth bill of the new Congress, creating a federal lighthouse system and making lighthouse management one of the principal activities of the U.S. government. (Gerry later was to be immortalized for carving out an electoral district in favor of his own party while governor, a tactic still called "gerrymandering.") The first public works law of the new nation, the bill was passed by the House on July 20 and by the Senate on July 31. President George Washington signed it on August 7, 1789.

"All expenses which shall accrue from and after the fifteenth day of August, 1789, in the necessary support, maintenance and repairs of all lighthouses, beacons, buoys and public piers erected, placed or sunk before the passing of this act, at the entrance of or within any bay, inlet, harbor, or port of the United States, for rendering the navigation thereof easy and safe shall be defrayed out of the treasury of the United States," it said. Lighthouse taxes would no longer be collected, and lighthouses would become symbols of the federal presence in the states.

The states were generally quick to hand over their existing lighthouses. Connecticut did so in May 1790, Massachusetts in June; Portland Head Light would be completed under congressional jurisdiction, making it both the last colonial light and the first federal one. Rhode Island, on the other hand, was stubborn, refusing to give up control of Beavertail Light, even after Congress gave it an ultimatum in the form of a follow-

up law in March 1790. "None of the said expenses shall continue to be so defrayed by the United States after the expiration of one year from the date aforesaid unless such lighthouse beacons, buoys and public piers shall in the meantime be ceded to and vested in the United States by the state or states," impatient lawmakers declared. Rhode Island finally relinquished Beavertail Light in May 1793, and even then with a proviso that if it were not maintained as an active navigational aid, the state would take it back.

With its authority now finally established, the government vastly accelerated the construction of new lights. Between 1789 and 1820, the number of lighthouses increased from twelve to fifty-five, helping enable U.S. shippers to establish fabulously profitable trade routes to the East Indies, China, Russia, and the Far East. And while the War of 1812 halted maritime commerce again, the U.S. fleet emerged to dominate the world's oceans, thanks to fast, sleek clipper ships, most of them built in New England.

Many contracts for the lighthouses that would guide these clippers from their wharves and safeguard trading vessels in and out of port were personally approved by Alexander Hamilton, the first secretary of the treasury, and by Washington and later presidents, who took a close interest in the lights. Local residents quickly realized the interest and authority of the federal government. When entreaties to the governor for a lighthouse on Cape Cod went nowhere, the Massachusetts Humane Society and the Boston Marine Society appealed directly to Congress. Citing the large number of shipwrecks off Cape Cod, the Reverend James Freeman wrote: "A lighthouse, should Congress think proper to erect one, would prevent many of these fatal accidents." Lawmakers in 1796 ordered the construction of Highland (Cape Cod) Light, which was finished in less than a year. Some New Englanders, however, preferred to simply ignore the government. East Chop (Telegraph Hill) Light on Martha's Vineyard, for example, was put up in 1869 by a ship captain who took the unusual step of asking for donations from marine insurance firms, shipping companies, residents, and merchants, and built the light himself.

The dominance of the northeastern United States in shipping was reflected in the location of new lights. Of the fourteen lighthouses built between the end of the Revolutionary War and 1799, all but four were north of New York City. So were all but six of the twenty-six lighthouses built in the following twenty years. By 1820, 75 percent of the nation's lighthouses were located be-

With poor planning and lackluster oversight, many early American lighthouses were so badly built they almost immediately had to be replaced. The first Pemaquid Point Light, built in 1827 in Maine, for example, quickly fell into ruin, apparently because the builder used salt water in the mortar mix. The lighthouse was replaced in 1835 by the existing thirty-eight-foot stone tower. The site is known for the extraordinary striations in the coastal rock.

tween the Delaware Bay and northern Maine.

But there were problems with the federal administration of the lighthouse system. Even after Congress did approve a lighthouse, there were maddening delays while local interests argued over where to put it. Money for a light in Scituate, Massachusetts, was approved in 1810, but it took more than a year for residents to agree to build it on the north side of the harbor. Politics would also come to play a role. When the powerful congressional delegation representing Maine pushed for lighthouse after lighthouse, a critic observed: "It seemed that nothing was ever turned down pertaining assistance to navigation on the coast."

Patronage and nepotism both were constants also. General Benjamin Lincoln, who, as customs collector for Boston, also supervised the region's lights, gave his son the contract to build Highland Light. Jonathan Nash, the first keeper at Watch Hill Light in Rhode Island, was unceremoniously sacked after twenty-seven years, in 1834, and replaced by a supporter of President Andrew Jackson. When President Zachary Taylor was elected in 1849, one of his supporters, Collins Howers, was promised the position of keeper of Chatham Light in Massachusetts. Only a community outcry saved the job for the much-loved widow of the previous keeper, who had inherited the post and needed it to feed her family. At Boon Island Light in Maine, John Thompson was fired in 1843 in favor of a patronage appointee, a former tailor who had barely ever seen the ocean. "I have been a seaman from a boy—being now sixty years old—am poor, have a family to support, with little or no means," Thompson

implored in a letter to Vice President John Tyler. "I voted for your excellency for vice president, and intended to exert my feeble influence to promote another election for you for president. Why I am removed, I am at a loss to determine." But Thompson had to wait through two more presidential administrations before he got his job back in 1849.

Stephen Pleasonton

By far the biggest problem of the Lighthouse Establishment was the man who ran it for much of the first half of the nineteenth century: Stephen Pleasonton, a penny-pinching bureaucrat in the Treasury Department, which was responsible for building and maintaining the lights. Pleasonton, who began in the job in 1820 and stayed for more than thirty years, had no maritime background or experience in maritime affairs. In addition to his lighthouse duties, he was also responsible for diplomatic and consular bank accounts and funding for the State Department, Patent Office, Census Bureau, and Boundary Commission. He had only nine clerks under him and relied on regional customs collectors to select and purchase lighthouse sites, oversee construction, and conduct an annual inspection. Most knew as little about lighthouses as Pleasonton did.

A notorious skinflint, Pleasonton required his personal approval for any expenditure over $100. He bragged that he returned allocations for the construction and repair of lighthouses to the treasury unspent and, in 1842, proudly told Congress that the U.S. Lighthouse Establishment was run at half the cost of its British counter-

The first lighthouse station in America, the Boston Light on Boston Harbor's Little Brewster Island remains the only staffed lighthouse in the United States.

The first sight of America seen by many transatlantic ships, Fire Island Light was nonetheless deactivated in 1974. Rescued by preservationists, it was reactivated in 1986.

part. But there was growing dissatisfaction with the lighthouses. Many had been built of wood and were so close to the waterline that they immediately rotted. Mortar had been mixed with sea water by careless contractors, causing lighthouse towers to crumble and have to be rebuilt. At Matinicus Rock Light in Maine, the first two sets of towers, built in 1827, were too short and close together to be distinguished at sea. They had to be replaced. Within ten years, they had to be replaced again. When an inspector visited Wing's Neck Light in Massachusetts, which was supposed to have been finished, he was steered to a local tavern by the contractor while workers hurriedly placed planking over barrels where the floor had yet to be laid. Finally arriving at the tower, he stepped on the end of a plank and fell to the foundation, injuring himself.

Yet even Pleasonton's famous miserliness couldn't save him from falling for a shady former sea captain who conned him—and his lighthouse department—into what would prove its worst mistake.

Born in Wellfleet, Massachusetts, the son of a sea captain, Winslow Lewis followed in his father's footsteps, becoming a captain himself at age thirty-five and commanding the twenty-three-ton merchant ship *Sally*. Idled in 1807 by the Jefferson embargo that would lead to the War of 1812, Lewis helped found the Boston Sea-Fencibles, mariners organized to defend Boston's islands and waterfront, and named himself commander. He also tried his hand as an inventor, patenting a light that made it possible to read a compass on a ship at night. Then Lewis took an interest in lighthouse lanterns, experimenting in the cupola of the Massachusetts State House with a way to make the beacon brighter and more visible to ships at sea.

On June 8, 1810, Lewis patented his "reflecting and magnifying lantern"—in fact, a barely concealed imitation of a type of lamp that had been invented in 1780 in Switzerland, which he combined with a convex reflector that had been developed around the same time in England. Lewis's lamp was poorly made, but what impressed Pleasonton was that it used only half the whale oil of existing models. He immediately purchased the dubious patent for the then-princely sum of $20,000, plus a share in the oil saved, and hired Lewis to install and maintain the devices in all forty-nine lighthouses then in operation. In 1816, Lewis also won a contract from Pleasonton to supply all the oil. He soon became the principal builder of new lighthouses in the United States

and the leading contractor for refitting old lights.

But the lighthouses Lewis built were as poor as his lamp was dim. The so-called Three Sisters Lights on Cape Cod, for example, were so sloppily constructed that the lantern rooms were tilted, and the Boston Customs office refused to accept the work. Lewis rushed to Washington ahead of the report and persuaded Pleasonton to pay him anyway. By now, Pleasonton relied heavily on Lewis. Lewis's own nephew, Isaiah William Penn Lewis, his greatest critic, complained that his uncle was allowed by Pleasonton to prepare specifications on new lighthouses and then bid on them himself. Lewis also resisted experimenting with other promising new fuels so he could keep his profitable monopoly on oil. More importantly, he thwarted the adoption of the considerably superior Fresnel lens then in use in Europe.

Isaiah Lewis tenaciously continued to demand changes. In 1842, thanks to a report he wrote about the neglected state of lighthouses in New England, he succeeded in persuading Congress to turn over control of several planned new lights to the U.S. Army Corps of Topographical Engineers, ushering in an age of new designs, materials, and construction techniques. By

Boston Light had to be refurbished to make room for this second-order Fresnel lens, which was installed in 1859. At the time, the tower was increased in height to eighty-nine feet.

It was thirty years after the establishment of Boston Light before another lighthouse was constructed in America: Brant Point Light, which went up at the entrance to Nantucket Harbor in 1746. Sea captains there had demanded a lighthouse, but would later balk at paying for it with a shipping tax. Today the lighthouse is decorated every Christmas.

The existing Brant Point Light, built in 1901, is the tenth on the site. The first burned down, the second was destroyed by a freak storm, and the rest were burned, consumed by rust, or left useless when the shipping channel shifted.

then, Congress was already fuming over an 1837 Board of Navy Commissioners report that thirty-one lighthouses planned by Pleasonton and Lewis were unnecessary. Navy officers were from then on assigned to inspect existing lighthouses and select sites for any new ones. In 1838, Congress sent Commander Matthew Perry, who later became famous for opening U.S. trade relations with Japan, to inspect Fresnel lenses in lighthouses in Europe. He was wildly enthusiastic. Still Pleasonton resisted, saying that more testing was needed and the Fresnel lenses were too complicated for keepers to operate. But his power was starting to slip. In 1845, two Navy officers toured European lighthouses yet again and told Congress they were much brighter and better maintained.

Finally, in 1851, Congress appointed a board of military officers and engineers and civilian scientists to investigate the situation. Their 760-page report urged that the system be revamped and operated by a professional board. They also urged the immediate adoption of the Fresnel lens.

The Lighthouse Board

Pleasonton was through. On October 9, 1852, he was stripped of his authority for lighthouses with the creation of the nine-member U.S. Lighthouse Board, made up of three navy officers, three army engineers, and three civilians, one of them the secretary of the treasury. Among the members was Alexander Dallas Bache, great-grandson of Benjamin Franklin, a physicist from Girard College in Philadelphia who specialized in navigation. It was a signal that science would now be brought to bear in lighthouse operation. Some things didn't change, however: Placed in charge of determining locations for new lights was Bache's brother, Richard. Fresnel lenses were ordered to be installed in all new lighthouses and in existing towers that needed replacement lights. Many did need replacements, since Pleasonton had allowed them to become third rate. The towers were poorly situated, sloppily built, and badly maintained, and the lights themselves were dim.

The Lighthouse Board traded romance for standardized efficiency. It divided the country into twelve lighthouse districts, beginning with the First District in New England. Each was assigned an inspector who made constant visits. A central supply depot was established on Staten Island, where whale oil used in lighthouses was also tested. Clear rules and procedures were imposed for the first time and were published in a pamphlet entitled *Instructions and Directions to Guide Light-House Keepers and Others Belonging to the Light-House Establishment.* "Articles known as luxurious are forbidden to be provided" by supply tenders, it said, among other instructions. One of the board's first major projects, a replacement for a tower destroyed in a storm at Minot's Ledge in Massachusetts, was probably the greatest single engineering achievement of lighthouse construction, given the technology available. Greater standardization allowed the most successful designs to be used in more than one location. It was a marked contrast from Winslow Lewis's lopsided lights.

By 1884, uniforms were made standard for male keepers, consisting of doublebreasted coats with brass buttons and a cap with a yellow metal lighthouse badge above the visor.

But after its early successes, the Lighthouse Board started slowing down by the early 1900s. Some people complained that it was dominated by the military. On July 1, 1903, Congress transferred the board from the Treasury Department to the newly created Department of Commerce and Labor. On June 17, 1910, seeking to increase civilian control, Congress created the Bureau of Lighthouses, also known as the Lighthouse Service, and within two years civilians were in charge of nine of the twelve districts. In 1913, the bureau was assigned to the Department of Commerce when it split off from the Department of Labor.

The chief of the bureau was George R. Putnam, appointed as commissioner by President William Howard Taft; the two had met when Taft was governor of the Philippines and Putnam was coast survey director there. An engineer and adventurer who had been to Alaska, Greenland, and the Pacific, Putnam was, by all accounts, a good choice, running the bureau for twenty-five years until he retired in 1935.

Putnam introduced radio beacons, electric buoys, and electric fog signals, equipment that helped reduce the number of personnel needed. He created a retirement system for keepers, who had never had one. Congress passed a law in 1918 making bureau employees eligible for federal pensions. Putnam managed to increase the number of navigational aids from 11,713 in 1910 to 16,888 by 1924, while reducing the number of employees by 20 percent. He also inaugurated the monthly *Lighthouse Service Bulletin,* which contained, not only official news and information, but also recipes, instructions for whitewashing and pest extermination, monthly and regional forecasts, and even human-inter-

est stories about heroic rescues, tragedies, and station pets. Lights were also given other duties. Marshall Point Light in Maine, for instance, became one of the first connected by telephone to a local weather station, allowing it to display storm warning flags on a specially built mast. Sometimes during this era lighthouses were run by private contractors. New London Ledge Light, for instance, built in 1909, was maintained privately under contract to the Lighthouse Service until 1939.

By this time, shipping had begun to ebb in many older ports, and many lights went out. Maine's Dice Head Light, for example, was decommissioned because of a decline in shipping in Penobscot Bay. Plymouth (Gurnet) Light in Massachusetts almost met the same fate after commerce to Plymouth Harbor dropped off, but the opening of the Cape Cod Canal in 1914 gave it a new life as an important coastal beacon.

During the Depression, President Franklin Roosevelt's Reorganization Plan of 1939 transferred the administration of the lighthouses once again, this time from the Commerce Department to the Coast Guard. The transfer took effect July 1, 1939. Nationwide, more than 400 lighthouses, 30 lightships, and 64 lighthouse tenders were turned over within a week, along with 4,100 full-time and 1,200 part-time civilian employees, who were given the choice of remaining as civilians, of joining the Coast Guard, or of retiring. Nearly 500 keepers chose to join the Coast Guard, and were assigned the rank of chief petty officer or petty officer first class. District superintendents became commanders or lieutenant commanders, depending on seniority.

After World War II began, the Coast Guard—and, with it, the Lighthouse Service—was placed under the Navy Department for the duration. The war caused other drastic changes. Nineteen major and 1,227 minor lighthouses were turned off, and 91 reduced their power in a delicate tradeoff between coastal security and safety for the vital wartime convoys. Many became lookout stations. After the bombing of Pearl Harbor, the government began installing telephones in offshore lights, which were expected to watch for enemy submarines. This was not an idle threat. A British vessel was sunk by German torpedoes, and three U.S. ships were sunk by German U-boats—one on the very last day of the war—in view of Montauk Point Light in New York. Civil defense authorities built a two-story observation turret with small window slots atop one of the two towers at Cape Elizabeth Light in Maine to protect against possible infiltrators landed by submarine. Long Island's Horton

Point Light, which had been deactivated during the Depression, was recommissioned as a lookout for enemy aircraft.

After the war, to save money and remove its personnel from hazardous and isolated lights, the Coast Guard resumed the automation of the remaining 468 staffed lighthouses. Many keepers didn't want to go. Seventeen years later, in 1962, there were still 327 staffed lights. Soon the Coast Guard was facing increasing financial pressures as its responsibilities expanded to include illegal drug intervention, the cleanup of oil spills, and fisheries patrols with the enactment of the 200-mile fishing limit. In 1968, the Lighthouse Automation and Modernization Project, or LAMP, began in an effort to speed up the automation process.

Today there is only one staffed light in the United States: Old George Worthylake's Boston Light, still tended thanks to a 1989 act of Congress that states, "Boston Light will be forever manned." Occasional bumps in the night are excused with a shrug by the lonely Coast Guard complement of three. "Must be George," they like to say in homage to the nation's first keeper.

The Rhode Island legislature collected special levies from Newport shippers for eighteen years before finally building America's third lighthouse, Beavertail Light, in 1749.

Above: Many early lighthouses were ineffective. Mariners complained that Fire Island Light on Fire Island in New York was too short to be seen at sea. When a ship struck shoals and sank almost within sight of the lighthouse, Congress finally appropriated money for a higher tower. The current 180-foot lighthouse was completed in 1858.

Facing page: The Revolutionary War left local treasuries with little money for lighthouses. By 1787, when Massachusetts Governor John Hancock authorized the construction of Portland Head Light, he ordered it be built of cheap local field stones carried to the site by hand. The material turned out to be unexpectedly durable; the original lighthouse still stands. The lighthouse is in Maine, which was then a part of Massachusetts.

A rare triple light marked Eastham on Cape Cod beginning in 1838; the idea was to differentiate the spot from the twin lights at Chatham and the flashing Highland (Cape Cod) Light in Truro. Quickly nicknamed the Three Sisters, the first trio of towers were so badly built and inefficient they were torn down and replaced by three new wooden towers farther inland. Soon those, too, were on the brink of toppling into the sea, so they were discontinued and eventually retired to a clearing in the woods at the Cape Cod National Seashore.

The original Three Sisters Lights at Eastham on Cape Cod were an example of the shoddy workmanship—and political clout— of Winslow Lewis. The construction of the towers was so bad that local lighthouse service representatives refused to pay. Lewis rushed to Washington ahead of the report and got his money anyway. (Courtesy of the U.S. Coast Guard Historian's office)

In the nineteenth century, many lighthouse keepers were patronage appointees. Collins Howers, a supporter of President Zachary Taylor, for example, was promised the position of keeper of Chatham Light on Cape Cod. In this case, however, a community outcry saved the job for the much-loved widow of the previous keeper. Originally one of a number of twin lights along the north Atlantic coast, Chatham's pair of towers was broken up in 1923. The remaining lantern tower is decorated every Christmas.

In the early 1900s, as shipping began to ebb in many older ports, lighthouses started to be decommissioned. Dice Head Light, which had been built in 1828 to mark the mouth of the Penobscot River, went dark in 1937 with the decline of traffic on the river.

With comparatively little else to do, the early federal government made lighthouse building a surprisingly high priority. President George Washington himself called for the construction of Horton Point Light in Southold, New York, a settlement he had visited in 1757 during the French and Indian War. Decommissioned during the Depression in 1933, Horton Point was briefly revived as a lookout for enemy aircraft during World War II. It was permanently reactivated on its bicentennial in 1990.

CHAPTER 2

Rising Lights:

How the Lighthouses Were Built and How They Worked

Left: There was little science involved in deciding where to locate early lighthouses—or how to build them. Almost as soon as it was finished, Portland Head Light in Maine was found to be obstructed by a headland. When the sloping tower was increased in height, the lantern room ended up too narrow for the lamp.

Above: Lighthouse construction was often poor. Point Judith Light in Rhode Island is the third on this site, preceded by a wooden tower almost immediately destroyed in a hurricane, then a stone tower built so badly that it had to be replaced within two years.

The most significant wreck to come ashore on Nantucket in the seventeenth century was not a ship. It was a whale. Like other settlers along the northeast coast, Nantucketers were stuck with sandy soil and, in their case, a lack of wood for heat or shelter. Spinning and weaving were the principal businesses, and they provided only meager income. But when that dazed leviathan washed up on shore, it marked the start of an entirely new and extraordinarily profitable industry: hunting whales in the waters near the island for their oil.

Another chance encounter occurred in 1712, when a Nantucket whaler, Captain Christopher Hussey, found himself blown off course and far at sea. There he happened on a school of whales like none he had ever seen. They were sperm whales as long as 100 feet, and when he managed to harpoon one, he discovered that it yielded a vastly larger quantity of oil that was exceptionally pure.

This accident of fate would make Nantucket the whaling capital of the world. Its ships sailed the globe for sperm whales and their oil. The island's entire economy came to revolve around the business. By 1730, there were 25 whaling ships based at Nantucket, the start of a fleet that would grow to 200. It became the world's largest whaling port, and Massachusetts' third most populous town, after Boston and Salem.

But the entrance to Nantucket Harbor was a narrow one, and captains of broad ships filled with whale oil after years at sea became exasperated navigating just the last few hundred yards. In a crowded meeting hall on January 24, 1746, under lanterns lit by whale oil, they demanded that a lighthouse be constructed. Despite their Yankee thrift, the leaders of the town, dependent on the whalers for their growing affluence, agreed.

The sum of 200 pounds was appropriated, and three men got the job of building a squat wooden lighthouse, which was activated for the first time April 28, 1746. Over the next forty-two years, Nantucket would go through five lights destroyed due to fires, storms, and poor design. Four more lights would be built before 1901, when a wooden tower went up. Though the sea threatened to demolish it, 500 tons of rock were placed around it. Against all odds, it still stands.

But Nantucketers would not be the last to learn that building a lighthouse is harder than it looks.

Siting and Building the Lights

The first lighthouse in recorded history was the Tower of Pharos at the harbor in Alexandria, Egypt, which stood for more than 1,000 years. No wonder it is considered one of the seven wonders of the ancient world.

Lighthouses are exposed to extraordinarily savage seas, unrelenting winds, lightning, fires, and the corrosive effects of salt water. In the North Atlantic, they also suffer sub-zero temperatures in winter. How powerful is nature on the northeastern coast? A gale of fifty miles per hour pushing up against a lighthouse exerts a constant ten pounds of pressure per square inch, a typical hurricane twenty-six pounds per square inch, and an extraordinarily destructive hurricane forty-six pounds per square inch. During a storm in 1842, a fifty-seven-ton boulder near Mount Desert Rock Light in Maine was tossed across the island by the ocean like a toy. Massive granite blocks weighing several tons apiece and meant to reinforce the lighthouse on Maine's Boon Island were easily cast aside by waves. Nor was the original wood-framed lighthouse there any match for the elements, which wiped it off the face of the earth less than four years after it was built. The stone tower that replaced it was destroyed by a storm that produced waves so high they stopped up the chimneys of the keeper's house with seaweed. Seguin Island Light in Maine, also built of wood, was rotting away within five years, thanks to the salt air, and had to be replaced by a stone tower; even that could not withstand the gales. Waves of 60 feet have been recorded scouring the Minot's Ledge Light in Massachusetts, and the seas actually crashed over the 114-foot tower in a storm on November 25, 1888. The top of the seemingly indestructible granite Petit Manan Light in Maine was loosened by gales in 1886 and began to break away. It had to be reinforced by iron tie-rods, but it still swayed so violently in the wind that the weights that rotated the lantern broke away and fell to the foundation, taking with them most of the cast-iron spiral stairway.

It didn't help that many lighthouses on the East Coast were cheaply constructed and poorly maintained during the tenure of Stephen Pleasonton, the Treasury Department bureaucrat responsible for the Lighthouse Establishment during much of the first half of the 1800s. Pleasonton liked to boast that he returned much of the money allocated for the construction and repair of lighthouses to the treasury unspent. The worst debacles were the towers built by Winslow Lewis, a sea captain who used his friendship with the impressionable Pleasonton to become the principal builder of lighthouses in the United States. Lewis's workers ignored building specifications for the original Three Sisters Lights at Nauset in Massachusetts, for example, while the construction fore-

The encroachment of people has prompted alterations to lighthouses in the Northeast. To avoid confusion with house lights on Nantucket, Brant Point's white light was changed to red in 1933.

man looked the other way. Maine's Owl's Head Light was built with mortar mixed with salt water; almost immediately it began to deteriorate. The same thing happened at Pemaquid Point and West Quoddy Head Lights, also both in Maine; each lasted less than eight years.

Under Pleasonton's direction, regional customs collectors with little or no knowledge of building or maritime navigation made disastrous decisions about where and how to build lighthouses. Locations for lights often became dependent on whether there was also land for the keeper to farm, as at Highland (Cape Cod) Light on Cape Cod. There was little science involved. Highland ended up obstructed from the south because there were hills and woods in the way. It had to be raised. So did Owl's Head, which was originally only fifty-six feet above sea level. Mariners also complained that Fire Island Light in New York was too short, especially after the schooner Elizabeth struck the shoals and sank off the south coast of Long Island, drowning many of the crew; the captain said he had been looking for the light at the time. It was quickly doubled in height in response to the resulting outcry. The first light at New Haven's Five Mile Point was only thirty-five feet high, too short to be seen over a line of trees along the northeast and southeast shores. Gay Head Light on Martha's Vineyard was obscured 75 percent of the time. The original lighthouse at Marblehead, Massachusetts, was not much higher than a house and was blocked by summer cottages; the keeper had to put up a 100-foot mast and hang a lantern from it every night. And as soon as it was finished, Portland Head Light in Maine was discovered to be obstructed by a neighboring headland. When the height of the sloping tower was extended twenty feet, the lantern room ended up too narrow for the lamp. Even that was not the end of the fiasco. The tower was later lowered twenty feet, only to be raised again by twenty feet the next year.

But for every story of corruption and incompetence there are even more examples of ingenuity, bravery, and skill among the men who built the lights. Perhaps the most respected was John J. McComb, Jr., the architect who designed New York City Hall. His sturdy Eatons

Nature and neglect also took their toll. Built in 1901, the existing Brant Point Light required renovations in 1983 and again in 1992. One of its many predecessors became so rusted that it had to be replaced in 1856. An inspector visiting the lighthouse also found "the lantern smoked, lamps not trimmed, and reflectors looking as if weeks or months had elapsed since they had been cleaned."

Monhegan Island Light was the work of the architect Alexander Parris, who also designed Boston's Quincy Market. Along with the surrounding village, it has long been a favorite of artists.

Lichen on the sturdy granite tower at Monhegan Island Light

Neck and Montauk Point Lights on Long Island were built to last; the foundation at Montauk is thirteen feet deep with walls of Connecticut sandstone nine feet thick at the base. Both of these lights still stand, largely unchanged, after more than 200 years.

McComb was not the only famous architect to try his hand at lighthouse building. Alexander Parris, who designed Boston's Quincy Market, also was responsible for Execution Rocks Light in New York and Mount Desert Rock and Monhegan Island Lights in Maine. Castle Hill Light in Rhode Island is attributed to H. H. Richardson, famous for Trinity Church in Boston and the New York State Capitol.

But lighthouses weren't built for their looks. Most are circular because that is the shape that offers the least resistance to the wind and waves; tapered for stability;

and tall so they'll be visible at sea. The earliest were made of wood, simply because it was available. Around 1820, cut stones began to be used for the first time, allowing the towers to grow taller because the weight could be more evenly distributed. Granite became a particularly popular ingredient of Northeast lights thanks to the abundance of quarries.

With the increase in maritime trade after the War of 1812, the pace of lighthouse construction picked up dramatically, forcing some designs to be reused. The popular configuration for twin lights incorporated one tower at each end of a keeper's house, as at Bakers Island Light in Massachusetts and Matinicus Rock Light in Maine. Block Island North Light in Rhode Island, Plum Island and Old Field Point lights in New York, and Morgan Point, Sheffield Island (Norwalk), and Great Captain Island lights in Connecticut also share a single configuration: a tower standing like a steeple at the front of a peaked-roof keeper's house. Marshall Point and Isle Au Haut (Robinson Point) lights in Maine have matching towers and similar keeper's houses.

Only occasionally was there an effort to match the appearance of a lighthouse to its neighborhood. On Block Island, for example, the keeper's house at Southeast Light was built of red brick in a Victorian Gothic design with a steep gabled roof to correspond with the island's nineteenth-century architecture.

Beginning in the 1870s, some offshore lights took the odd-looking form of houses built on masonry foundations that served as their own tiny islands. Penfield Reef Light in Connecticut, for instance, was a two-story house with white trim mounted on a freestanding granite pier with the tower jutting from the roof. Rose Island Light in Rhode Island was a frame house with a mansard roof on a circular foundation. Stepping Stones Light in New York—set 1,600 yards offshore—is a lonely red brick house with granite trim, fronted by a square light tower. The same design was used to build the Colchester Reef Light on Lake Champlain in Vermont, which often proved as inhospitable as the Atlantic. Perhaps the most eccentric lighthouse in the Northeast is the red brick New London Ledge Light, a mile off the coast of Connecticut, which looks like a house that broke off and floated away from nearby New London. The light tower rises from the center of the mansard roof like a cupola.

One of the greatest engineering feats was New York's Race Rock Light, near Fishers Island at the entrance to

Monhegan Island Light is now part of the Monhegan Museum, which uses it to house historical mementos, including the American flag that covered the coffin of a lighthouse keeper's son who died while fighting in the Civil War.

Long Island Sound, which was built on a ledge exposed only at low tide. The ledge was deadly to shipping traffic; eight vessels were lost to it in the eight years before construction on a lighthouse finally began in April 1871. Beacons and buoys had been tried before that, but all had been swept away. Even so, it had taken a skeptical Congress forty years to appropriate the money for a lighthouse, which was to have been built on a nearby spit of land. But when a study found it would have inadvertently directed vessels straight across the treacherous reef, and not away from it, plans began for the seemingly impossible task of building a lighthouse on the ledge itself. It took seven years, 10,000 tons of granite blocks, and the $268,000 budget earmarked for the entire project just to build the sixty-nine-foot-diameter oval foundation. Masons had to work in water thirteen feet deep at low tide; two workmen were killed. But when the stylish two-story keeper's house was built atop this base, it was hailed as a feat of engineering genius.

Only two other lighthouses would be built this way:

New London Ledge and Stratford Shoal (Middle Ground) Lights in Connecticut. It was precisely the expense and difficulty of these lights that led the Lighthouse Board to a new building material: cast iron. Hollow rings of iron could be safely sunk in shallow water and filled with sand, rock, or concrete to form a base for a lighthouse, often also made of iron. Comparatively cheap, cast iron was also watertight and resisted corrosion. More than fifty lighthouses of this type would be built nationwide.

The nation's first cast-iron caisson and tower was Duxbury Pier ("Bug") Light in Massachusetts, built in 1871 to mark an offshore shoal. Inside the fat, squat tower was a three-level living area with a watch deck on the fourth floor, continuing a trend toward combining living and lighthouse functions that had begun with the advent of the Lighthouse Board in 1852. As this economical design became more popular, it began to be used all over the East Coast, including in five lighthouses in Connecticut and one in New York. The same plans and specifications could be recycled at each site. Most of the cast-iron lights have proved as durable as advertised, though cracks in the foundation of Orient Point Light in New York, also called Old Coffee Pot, have caused a five-degree tilt, and the cast-iron tower at Stratford Point Light in Connecticut was often struck by lightning.

So proud were they of this design, lighthouse planners displayed Connecticut's Southwest Ledge (New Haven Breakwater) Light at the 1876 Centennial Exposition in Philadelphia before installing it off New Haven the next year. They also started to incorporate cast iron in onshore lights, including East Chop (Telegraph Hill) Light on Martha's Vineyard. Nobska Point Light in Massachusetts consisted of an iron shell cast near Boston and shipped to the site in four sections. The Portland Breakwater ("Bug") Light in Maine, a wooden tower that quickly rotted because it was only two feet above high tide, was replaced with a cast-iron lighthouse that looks like a Greek monument, complete with Corinthian columns.

The most challenging conditions, of course, continued to demand unique materials and designs. Graves Light in Boston Harbor, for example, required massive blocks of granite to be cut on shore, ferried to the wave-swept ledge that served as the foundation of the lighthouse, and fitted together there by masons. The shoal was completely submerged at high tide, limiting the time work could proceed. It was two years before the light was activated on September 1, 1905. Ram Island Ledge in Portland Harbor was built the same way at the same time. It required 700 granite blocks that each weighed four tons.

As shipping patterns changed, some lighthouses were simply transplanted. Rhode Island's original Goat Island Light was dismantled in 1851 and moved ten miles from Newport to Portsmouth. Two of Winslow Lewis's poorly built Three Sisters Lights were sold, moved to new sites, and converted into summer cottages. The third was replaced in 1923 by one of nearby Chatham's twin light towers. Stonington Harbor Light in Connecticut was moved stone by stone in 1840 from one side of the harbor to the other. What is now the Edgartown Harbor Light on Massachusetts' Chappaquiddick Island was moved there by barge from Ipswich in 1939.

Erosion also forced the relocation of many coastal lights. Block Island North Light in Rhode Island, built in 1829, had to be replaced in 1837, in 1857, and again in 1867, when it was finally rebuilt hundreds of yards inland. One of the twin towers at Chatham Light on Cape Cod toppled into the sea in 1879, followed by the second tower in 1881. Fortuitously, cast-iron replacements had been erected farther inland just before that time. Shifting sands were constantly moving not only the ground beneath the Newburyport Harbor (Plum Island) Light in Massachusetts but also the Merrimac River channel that the lights marked. In 1887, even the construction of a replacement tower had to be abandoned, so quickly had the river shifted.

Sometimes the process worked in reverse. Cedar Island in New York shrank from three acres to less than an acre before a 6,000-ton breakwater was added to protect the lighthouse there. Then the hurricane of September 21, 1938, unexpectedly filled in the strait and made the island a peninsula. At Monomoy Point off Cape Cod, the lighthouse built to overlook treacherous coastal shoals found itself uselessly landlocked in the middle of a sandy island that had gradually formed around it. It was deactivated in 1923.

The newest lights are even more economical than their cast-iron predecessors. They may be skeletal towers with airport-style plastic beacons, or even vertical poles. They also take advantage of existing buildings. In Beverly, Massachusetts, for example, there is a rear range light in the First Baptist Church steeple (the front range light is at Hospital Point) to help guide vessels along the main ship channel into Salem.

The Lamps

The first rudimentary aid to navigation on Ram Island Ledge in Maine was a lantern in a moored dory. The problem was most mariners never actually saw the light until they had collided with the dory.

Building a lighthouse seemed easy compared to finding a light source bright enough to be seen at sea—especially in the candle-powered eighteenth century. The weak light of some tallow candles was, in fact, the only beacon from the earliest towers, including Plymouth (Gurnet) Light in Massachusetts. It was woefully inadequate.

In the late 1700s, some lighthouses switched to the bucket or "spider" lamp, a crude type of lantern that consisted of four or more wicks protruding from a pan of whale oil. First used in the United States at Boston Light in 1790, spider lamps gave off acrid fumes. They also needed tending several times a night to replenish the oil, to trim the wicks, and to clean the heavy smoke and soot from the glass. Spider-lamp keepers, nicknamed "wickies" because of the amount of time they spent tending to the wicks, also had to remember to cover the lanterns in the morning so they wouldn't be re-ignited by the rays of the rising sun. One keeper, at Highland (Cape Cod) Light, would forget to turn his wicks down and find them burning again by noon. Some wickies were noted for not cleaning the glass. A check of Portland Head Light in Maine discovered the glass so neglected that the beacon was almost impossible to see through the heavy film of soot. An inspector visiting Brant Point Light on Nantucket found "the lantern smoked, lamps not trimmed, and reflectors looking as if weeks or months had elapsed since they had been cleaned, they were so black and spotted."

But more advances lay on the horizon. William Hutchinson, an Englishman, invented a silver-coated parabolic reflector that could concentrate a beam of light. Then the Swiss inventor François-Pierre Ami Argand developed the Argand lamp, the first true modern light source. It consisted of an oil lamp with a wick enclosed in two concentric glass tubes above a reservoir of oil. The tubes circulated oxygen to feed the flame, which was equivalent to seven candlepower. A lighthouse might use as many as thirty of these lamps, for a total of about 200 candlepower. It was the brightest light known up to that time.

Although Hutchinson's reflector was invented in 1763 and Argand's lamp in 1780, neither was immediately introduced in the United States. Under the direction of Stephen Pleasonton, the Lighthouse Establishment accepted Winslow Lewis's cheap copy, a "reflecting and magnifying lantern" for which Lewis had somehow won a patent. His polishing solution, an abrasive cleaner called Tripoli powder, rubbed away the silver coating, and the lamps were so heavy they wore out the underlying tracks. Poorly assembled, they were also quickly jostled out of focus. Yet Pleasonton bought the patent and had the lamps installed in every lighthouse in the United States by 1817. It would take another forty-five years to get rid of them all.

Complaints began to pour in immediately. Mariners griped that the lamp at Race Point Light on Cape Cod was too dim for passing ships to see. At Petit Manan in Maine, the light was so weak it was rarely visible from a distance. But Lewis resisted experimenting with gas or other promising light sources since he had the contract to supply the oil to the lights. A single beacon could consume as much as 1,800 gallons of top-grade strained whale oil annually. At about one dollar a gallon in the

A granite house with a lantern tower attached at the front like a church steeple, Morgan Point Light in Connecticut used the same design as several other Northeast lighthouses. It is now a private home.

mid-nineteenth century, it was by far the largest single expense of operating a lighthouse.

Keepers also grumbled about the quality of the oil they received from Lewis. Thinner oil that should have gone to lighthouses in warmer states was sent to the Northeast, where it congealed in the cold. "Perhaps a few lives would be saved if better oil was provided," the keeper of Highland Light told the author Henry David Thoreau. The keeper, Thoreau recorded on a visit, "spoke of the anxiety and sense of responsibility which he felt in cold and stormy nights in the winter, when he knew that many a poor fellow was depending on him and his lamps burned dimly, the oil being chilled."

The matter reached a crisis in the late 1850s, when the price of whale oil quadrupled, and the government began to search for alternate fuels. By 1867, lard oil was being used in larger lights, and mineral oil was tried in some others, including Point Judith in Rhode Island. The Lighthouse Bureau also experimented with oil from fish, porpoises, olives—even wild cabbage seeds. Gas was tried, but proved difficult to supply because the pipes eroded. Beginning in 1877, kerosene was tested in small lights. The kerosene was heated, and its vapor formed a glowing ball, the same principle used in modern camp lanterns.

Electricity was slow to be adopted, mainly because most coastal lights were far from power sources. The first use of electricity came in 1886 with the placing of an arc light in the Statue of Liberty, which is technically an aid to navigation. But most lighthouses were not converted until the 1920s and 1930s. Block Island South-

Above: *Built on the dramatic Monhegan Bluffs to help guide ships around the treacherous southeast tip of Block Island, Southeast Light was threatened by erosion and deactivated in 1990. Volunteers raised $2 million and accomplished the seemingly impossible job of moving the lighthouse 300 feet from the edge of bluffs; it was relit in 1994.*

Right: *Possibly the most eccentric lighthouse in the Northeast, New London Ledge Light looks like a house that broke off and floated away from nearby New London, Connecticut, ending up a mile out to sea.*

east Light was not electrified until 1928 and Highland Light until 1932.

Even after it was widely used, electricity was not always reliable. When Marblehead Light in Massachusetts failed during the hurricane of 1938, the keeper, Harry S. Marden, drove his car up to the lighthouse, connected the battery to the tower's fuse box, and kept the lantern running that way until dawn.

Lenses

Like the lights themselves, lighthouse lens technology advanced in Europe far ahead of the United States. In 1822, a French physicist named Augustin Fresnel invented a superior beehive-style glass lens that completely encircled the lamp, with refracting prisms at the top and bottom and bullseye-style magnifying panes around the middle to direct the light into a solid bright beam. There are seven sizes, or "orders," of Fresnel lenses, from a first-order lens (the largest, at about 7 feet, 10 inches in height and 6 feet in diameter) to a sixth-order lens (the smallest, at 1 foot, 5 inches tall and about 1 foot wide), plus a three-and-a-half-order lens. The mechanism often rested on a bed of mercury so that it could be turned easily, usually by hanging weights similar to those used in grandfather clocks.

So advanced was the Fresnel lens that it is still in use today, though most contemporary models are made of cheaper plastic; at current prices, a first-order Fresnel glass lens would cost about $7 million. But Pleasonton, prodded by Lewis, refused to adopt them, in spite of the entreaties of ships' captains who had seen how bright they made the lights in Europe. The lens was too expensive, Pleasonton responded—though engineers said it would pay for itself through the savings in oil. When Congress sent Commander Matthew Perry to Europe in 1938 to visit lighthouses with Fresnel lenses, he was so impressed he purchased two of them for tests. By order of Congress, they were installed at Highland and Sankaty Head Lights in Massachusetts in 1840 to wide acclaim. Fishermen called Sankaty Head "the blazing star" and said it was so bright they could bait their hooks by it. And yet, in 1842, Pleasonton ordered the Fresnel lens removed from Highland Light and Lewis's Argand-style lamp returned. He claimed the lenses were too complicated for the keepers to operate and needed more testing.

After thwarting the use of state-of-the-art lamps for decades, Pleasonton finally lost his authority over the lighthouse system. When the U.S. Lighthouse Board was created in 1852, military officers, engineers, and scientists started to experiment with new designs, materials, fuels, technology, and methods. By 1859, superior Fresnel lenses had been installed in every major lighthouse in the United States.

Distinguishing the Beacons

No matter how bright the beacons, lighthouses were of little use unless a ship could tell one from another. This became evident almost as soon as lighthouses began to be built in North America, when Plymouth (Gurnet) Light in Massachusetts began to be confused with nearby Boston Light. In an attempt to set them apart, Plymouth Light was built with two towers instead of one, becoming the first so-called twin light in America. Seven other sets of twin lights would be built, six of them in New England: Cape Elizabeth and Matinicus Rock Lights in Maine; and Chatham, Thacher Island (Cape Ann), Bakers Island, and Newburyport Harbor (Plum Island) Lights in Massachusetts. There was also one triple light in the United States: Three Sisters Lights at Nauset on Cape Cod.

Double and triple lights proved to be, at best, stopgap measures. The twin towers at Plymouth Light were only thirty feet apart; from a distance, the two beacons appeared to merge into one. At Bakers Island Light, the towers were so close that the government extinguished one of them. Then, in 1817, the freighter *Union*, loaded with pepper, slammed into the island; the captain said he had mistaken Bakers Island Light for Boston Light. In 1820, after a second shipwreck, the second tower was reactivated. When the government darkened one of the two beacons at Cape Elizabeth Light in 1882, the protest was so great that the decision there also was reversed.

Soon after Highland Light was built on Cape Cod in 1797, sailors blown off course began confusing it, too, with Boston Light. So Highland was equipped with the first eclipsing mechanism in an American lighthouse: a blind that would pass in front of the light once a minute to distinguish it from the five fixed lights on the route to Boston. In practice, it only served to obscure the light much of the time.

Lighthouse planners continued to experiment. Lighthouses with fixed lights were called "steady," and flashing lights, "occulating." The intervals of flashing also varied. A beacon might flash dark for a shorter time than it would light, or light longer than dark, for instance. Race Point Light flashed once every ten seconds, nearby Highland Light once every five. Red or green glass was used to turn the lights a different color. Wood End Light

Built in 1871, Duxbury Pier ("Bug") Light in Massachusetts was America's first cast-iron "spark plug"–style offshore lighthouse. Inside is a three-level living area with a watch deck on the fourth floor. The economical design would come to be used all over the Northeast.

on Cape Cod became a flashing red, while neighboring Long Point Light showed a steady green. All of this caused more work for the keepers, who had to wind the rotating mechanism several times a night.

There continued to be problems. Before Minot's Ledge Light was constructed, captains often confused Scituate Light and Boston Light and ran directly into Minot's Ledge, for instance. Nantucket's Great Point Light was constantly mistaken for the Cross Rip and Handkerchief Shoal Lightships. By 1890, around the time a distinguishing red glass was finally added, more than forty-three shipwrecks had occurred beneath the sweep of Great Point's beacon.

With vessels often out to sea for months or even years, changes in these distinguishing features could be catastrophic. After New York's Shinnecock Light, which no longer stands, was activated on New Year's Day 1858,

Montauk Point Light—previously the only beacon on that stretch of coast—was changed from a steady beam to a flashing signal. Forty-nine days later, the ship *John Milton*, returning from San Francisco via Cape Horn, confused the two lights and smashed into the rocks. All thirty-three people aboard were drowned. To avoid such tragedies, the Lighthouse Board began the *Annual Light List*, which shows all lighthouses and their characteristics, with changes noted in periodic updates called "Notice to Mariners."

The encroachment of people also has prompted alterations to the lights. Brant Point's white light was changed to red in 1933 to avoid confusion with house lights. Watch Hill Light in Rhode Island was changed from a steady white beam to an intermittent red one to distinguish it from streetlights.

Above: *To lower construction costs, Nobska Point Light on Cape Cod was built of an iron shell cast near Boston in 1876 and shipped to the site in four sections.*

Left: *The challenging conditions of the Northeast coast made lighthouse construction unusually difficult. Building Ram Island Ledge Light in Portland Harbor in 1905 required 700 granite blocks each weighing four tons to be cut on shore, ferried to the wave-swept ledge that served as the foundation of the lighthouse, and fitted together there by masons. (Courtesy of Jeremy D'Entremont. Reprinted by permission of Dorothy Bicknell.)*

The Northeast's shifting shoreline made some lights obsolete. Monomoy Point Light on Cape Cod, for instance, built in 1849, soon found itself uselessly landlocked in the middle of a sandy island that had formed around it. It was finally deactivated in 1923.

Foghorns

The development of foghorns closely followed that of lighthouses, especially in the fogbound Northeast. The third keeper of Boston Light on Boston Harbor's Little Brewster Island asked that "a great gun be placed on the said island to answer ships in a fog." He was given a small cannon, America's first fog signal, which is preserved to this day on the campus of the U.S. Coast Guard Academy in New London, Connecticut.

It proved much harder to pierce the fog than to light the night. The first mention of a fog bell at West Quoddy Head Light in Maine came in 1820, but it was 1869 before the lighthouse—along with Cape Elizabeth and Matinicus Rock lights—was equipped with an adequate steam-powered fog whistle, the most powerful at the time. The foghorn at Seguin Island Light in Maine was so loud "its concussion has put out an oil lantern set on the ground eight feet below the horn itself," keeper Frank E. Bracey said. "I have seen seagulls which were flying by actually knocked down by the force of the concussion." The horn was so powerful it could be heard fourteen miles away in Bath. It had to be. Seguin Island is one of the foggiest places in the country; one year it was socked in more than 30 percent of the time, or a record 114 days.

Some of the nation's greatest minds tried to solve the problem of fog warnings. A team of students from the Massachusetts Institute of Technology lived on Little Brewster Island in the summer of 1893, experimenting with various foghorns in an unsuccessful attempt to pierce the mysterious area around a lighthouse called the ghost walk, which sound seemed not to penetrate. Fog signals were also tested at Beavertail Light in Rhode Island, including one powered by a horse on a treadmill. On Whitehead Island Light in Maine, the rising and falling tides wound a 2,000-pound weight-operated spring mechanism that powered the fog bell. Damaged by surf after two winters, the system was replaced with a steam whistle. Monhegan Island Light in Maine was on the highest point of land to maximize its beacon, but it was too far from the ocean for a fog signal, so a signal house was built along the shore and assigned a separate keeper, who communicated with the lighthouse by telegraph. At New London Harbor Light in Connecticut, a shrill siren was tried. Though one of the most effective fog signals ever tested, it was silenced by complaints from neighbors.

Neighbors often lobbied to have fog signals muted, as at Saybrook Breakwater Light in Connecticut, whose massive 1,000-pound fog bell would sometimes toll all night. Keepers weren't too crazy about them either. The bell tower at Stratford Point Light in Connecticut was struck every thirty seconds by a clockwork mechanism that ran for half an hour but took twenty minutes to wind.

It would prove only one of the countless hardships of the lonely Atlantic keeper.

Because of the difficulty of its construction, Ram Island Ledge Light was one of the last offshore lights made of anything other than cast iron. The lonely outpost was automated in 1959.

Monomoy Point Light is today surrounded by a national wildlife refuge.

Above: Race Point Light was built to help guide ships around the dangerous shallows at the tip of Cape Cod. The original wooden lighthouse here was wooden and had one of the earliest revolving beacons, but proved ineffective and was replaced in 1876 with this cast-iron tower.

Right: The original Highland (Cape Cod) Light was built far enough inland so the keeper could farm—but ended up obstructed from the south by hills and woods that blocked its beacon. It had to be raised. In 1996, when erosion brought the coastline so close that the 404-ton lighthouse was endangered, it was moved 450 feet to safety.

TRAGEDY AND TRIUMPH:
THE FALL AND RISE OF MINOT'S LEDGE LIGHT

*T*he frantic clanging of a fog bell could be heard on shore even above the terrible sound of the storm that churned the waters off Cohasset, Massachusetts, just before 1 A.M. on April 17, 1851. It was the sound of one of the worst lighthouse disasters in the history of the United States.

More than fifty wrecks and forty deaths had been blamed on the barely visible outcropping of rock called Minot's Ledge—so many that the Massachusetts Humane Society anchored the nation's first lightship at the ledge in 1807—before the government had finally agreed to build a lighthouse there in 1841.

The job was thought to be impossible—so complex that it was taken away from the politically connected contractors who built most of the lights in those days and given to the U.S. Army Corps of Topographical Engineers. Planners decided against using stone, believing it would be impossible to pile heavy granite blocks atop the narrow, seaswept ledge. Instead, they settled on a unique design that put the lighthouse, spiderlike, on legs of less-expensive iron pilings that would allow the powerful waves to pass beneath, instead of battering the tower.

Construction finally began in 1847 and took two years to complete. Work could proceed only on calm days during low tide. Heavy machinery was twice swept from the rocks. Slowly, nine holes, each five feet deep, were drilled into the ledge for the iron legs that would support the lighthouse. At the end of 1849, the lamp was lit.

The nation was impressed. But the first keeper, Isaac Dunham, wasn't. Dunham immediately reported that the sea "makes the lighthouse reel like a drunken man. I hope God will in mercy still the raging sea, or we must perish." His entreaties that the tower be strengthened only managed to insult the builder, Captain William H. Swift. "Time, the great expounder of the truth or the fallacy of the question, will decide for or against the Minot," Swift wrote in a letter to a Boston newspaper. "But inasmuch as the light has outlived nearly three winters, there is some reason to hope that it may survive one or two more."

Unwilling to test that theory, Dunham quit, to be replaced by John W. Bennett. After a howling nor'easter in the fall of 1850, Bennett, too, was warning that the lighthouse was in danger. But the committee assigned to inspect the tower arrived during a calm day and reported it was solid as a rock.

At 2 A.M. on Sunday, March 16, 1851, Bennett and assistant keepers, Joseph Wilson and Joseph Antoine, were awakened by a gale so strong they went down into the storeroom at the bottom of the lighthouse, fearing that the top would be sheared off. There they stayed for four days with

The overconfident designers of Minot's Ledge Light insisted that the power of the sea would pass harmlessly through its spiderlike legs. But the iron tower, completed in 1850, proved no match for the New England seas and was destroyed within a year. (Courtesy of the U.S. Coast Guard Historian's office)

the tower swaying so much that they could barely mount the ladder to the lantern room. Finally, the wind died down, and Bennett went to Boston to tell anyone who would listen that the lighthouse had been badly weakened.

Within a month, on Wednesday, April 16, 1851, another storm hit. Wilson and Antoine, alone at the light, kept the beacon lit; it could still be seen from shore as late as 10 P.M. But midnight would bring high tide. Already, the tower had begun to pitch back and forth as waves crashed against the upper structure, sixty feet above the ledge. Around 11 P.M., the central support snapped, and the top-heavy, thirty-ton, cast-iron lighthouse now was being held up only by its weakened outer pilings. An hour later, it was resting on the last two or three of its nine iron legs. The men inside were banging in a frenzy on the lighthouse bell, but there was no prospect of rescue. Soon the sound abruptly stopped; the tower was beneath the waves. Antoine's body washed ashore. Wilson made it as far as a rock outcropping, where he perished from exposure.

They did not die in vain. The disaster focused attention on the shoddy record of the Lighthouse Establishment and

If the first Minot's Ledge Light was an example of engineering folly, its replacement was one of the greatest achievements of American lighthouse construction. This time granite, instead of iron, was used, and the tower took shape from more than 1,000 dovetailed granite blocks ferried to the ledge from shore. (Courtesy of Jeremy D'Entremont. Reprinted by permission of Dorothy Bicknell.)

Using a rotating screen, Highland (Cape Cod) Light was the first in the nation to display a flashing light. The idea was to distinguish it from nearby fixed beacons, but the result was that the light was obscured much of the time. The original 1857 first-order Fresnel lens has also been removed and was largely destroyed in the process. Today, a modern plastic beacon shines from the lantern room.

hastened the creation of the new U.S. Lighthouse Board. The board immediately decided to replace the Minot's Ledge Light, in what turned out to be one of the triumphs of lighthouse engineering.

This time a stone tower, instead of iron, was planned. Construction began in 1855. The stumps of the first tower were removed, and a granite foundation was carefully measured and cut to tightly grip the ledge. More than 1,000 dovetailed granite blocks weighing 3,500 tons slowly rose above it. Conditions were treacherous. The entire first year's work was destroyed when the bark *New Empire* crashed against the framework in a storm on January 19, 1857. In all, the new light would take five years and $330,000 to complete.

Finally, on August 22, 1860, the lamp was lit. It was just a test. When the light was activated permanently three months later by keeper Joshua Wilder, the bright beacon was greeted with fireworks.

Minot's Ledge remains one of the most dangerous lighthouse sites in the United States. In a storm on November 25, 1888, the seas actually went over the 114-foot tower. On Christmas Day, 1909, a wave 170 feet high was reported. In winter, it's almost impossible to bring a boat alongside; even then, ice has to be hacked from the ladder that runs from the foot of the tower to the entry door forty feet above.

Today the lighthouse is automated and lit with solar power. But a monument on nearby Government Island, where the granite blocks were cut, memorializes the men who died while keeping the light.

Great Point Light replaced a beacon lit as early as 1769 to mark the tip of Nantucket Island.

The biggest single expense of operating a nineteenth-century lighthouse was the whale oil needed to fuel the lamp. Great Point Light on Nantucket used as much as 1,800 gallons of top-grade whale oil every year, at a cost of about one dollar a gallon—a fortune at the time.

Above: *The problem of confusing one light for another was blamed for countless shipwrecks off Nantucket, whose Great Point Light, built in 1818, was often mistaken for the Cross Rip or Handkerchief Shoal lightships. By 1890, a distinguishing red glass was finally added. The current seventy-foot lighthouse at this site is a modern-day replica of the 1818 original, which was destroyed by a storm in 1984.*

Facing page: *Saybrook Breakwater Light was built in 1886 of cast iron to help guide ships into the dredged deep channel. Mariners may have been grateful, but neighbors lobbied to have the massive 1,000-pound fog bell silenced. The lighthouse's exterior was restored by the Coast Guard in 1996, and it appears on Connecticut license plates as a symbol of preserving Long Island Sound.*

CHAPTER 3

Life in a Lighthouse:

The Lot of the Lighthouse Keeper

Left: Keepers lived in virtual isolation in lighthouses such as Curtis Island Light in Maine, which sits off the Camden Harbor entrance on Penobscot Bay.

Above: Lighthouse keepers often served at the whim of the times. The first keeper of Thacher Island (Cape Ann) Lights in Massachusetts was a Tory, who was removed at the outset of the Revolutionary War. The twin light towers and the keeper's house, right down to the raincoats hanging on the wall, have been preserved.

John Polereczky was an Alsatian count, born to a French noble family, who had volunteered to fight for the American revolutionary cause and became a major in the Continental Army. So it's understandable that, when he asked the government for a job after the war, he expected a dignified position.

Instead, he was made a lighthouse keeper, in his case at Maine's Seguin Island Light, an inhospitable outpost whose name comes from the Native American words for "place where the sea vomits."

It was an apt description. Polereczky's house immediately began to rot away in the salt air and finally was smashed in a storm. Wind and waves demolished three of his boats in succession, flooded his garden, and destroyed his barn. "There is no feed on the island," he complained to General Benjamin Lincoln, customs collector in Boston, on May 12, 1796. "I must carry two cows for my family and keep them on hay, summer and winter, which I must purchase and carry on the island, with the greatest difficulty. I must keep also a horse on hay to haul or carry my oil, provisions, firewood, etc. etc. I must purchase a good boar. I must purchase every individual necessity for my family till I can raise it."

Polereczky wanted an increase in his annual salary of $150, meager even then. But headquarters was unsympathetic. After all, the government responded, he was receiving free fuel, lived on public land, and could fish and raise a garden. The bureaucrats made one concession: They agreed to send a new boat.

"The salaries of keepers appear to have been subjected to some miscalculation on their part from the unnecessary degree of former standing which some of the candidates have had," wrote the revenue commissioner, who no doubt lived in a warm house far from harm's way. "It is plain at first view that the above duties are not in their nature adapted to the standing of a field officer, or of a major of brigade."

After five years on the island, Polereczky dropped dead, relieving him of his problems after all.

Such was the lot of the lighthouse keeper, a role romanticized by artists and poets but, in fact, a dismal life of loneliness, monotony, and deprivation punctuated with mortal danger and, occasionally, guilt.

The men—and many women—who held these jobs ranged from heroes to freeloaders. They boasted names like Sylvester Hazard of Beavertail Light in Rhode Island, Ebenezer Skiff at Gay Head Light in Massachusetts, Titus Salter of the Portsmouth Harbor Light in New Hampshire, and Ezekiel Darling, an ex-gunner on the USS *Constitution*, who kept Marblehead Light in Massachusetts. They were often proud of their role—and occasionally defensive of it. "It should be borne in mind that the adults on these scraggly islands and barren rocks are by no means lifelong recluses," declared Robert T. Sterling, who tended Great Duck Island Light in Maine. "Many of them lived in large cities before they entered the service and are no more unsophisticated than their fellow men nearer the centers of civilization."

In fact, many of the keepers came with the property. When the Massachusetts Bay Colony built Plymouth (Gurnet) Light in 1768 on land owned by John Thomas, for example, they simply made him keeper as part of the deal. Ditto Gershom Smith, who owned the site on which the government built Sheffield Island (Norwalk) Light in Connecticut (and whose son, Theodore, would later serve as acting head of the Lighthouse Board for several years). Connecticut's Five Mile Point Light was built on the spot where a farmer named Amos Morris had outwitted a British landing party one night during the Revolutionary War by mounting his horse and calling out orders to the rocks and trees as though they comprised a phalanx of defending troops. The British fled, but later they returned and burned down Morris's house and barn. When the lighthouse was constructed there in 1805, the government made Morris keeper, though he quit after only three weeks.

Keepers did not necessarily fade into obscurity after taking up their isolated posts. One of Amos Morris's successors at Five Mile Point, Captain Elizur Thompson, resigned after seven years and journeyed to Alaska to seek his fortune in the gold rush. He returned two years later, penniless but rich with stories for the visitors he welcomed after taking up his light-keeping job again. Captain Paul Pinkham, an early keeper of Great Point Light in Massachusetts, prepared the first accurate map of the New England coast in 1790, including the Nantucket Shoals and Georges Bank. And James W. Hinckley, assistant keeper at Race Point Light in Massachusetts, quickly tired of carrying heavy groceries two and a half miles across sand dunes, so he put balloon tires on a 1934 Ford, thereby apparently inventing the dune buggy.

A Bleak Existence

The isolation of many lighthouses certainly afforded time for these and other supplementary pursuits. The lights were often not only remote but also situated on desolate islands off the Northeast coast.

Many fit this description by the Lighthouse Board of Matinicus Rock in Maine: "There is neither tree nor shrub, and hardly a blade of grass. The surface is rough and irregular and resembles a confused pile of loose stone. Portions of the rock are frequently swept over by waves which move the huge boulders into new positions." Even landing on these islands required that the boater wait for a swell, steer for the boatway, and haul the boat to high ground before the next wave pulled it back to sea. The only way to get on and off Saddleback Ledge in Maine was on a bosun's chair connected to a hoist and boom, since high seas normally submerged the landing area—and, occasionally, the keeper's quarters.

Like Saddleback Ledge, Maine's Mount Desert Rock and Boon Island were so inhospitable that soil had to be brought there from the mainland in burlap bags to grow vegetables. Most of the time, it was washed away. Mount Desert Rock came to be known as God's Rock Garden; George Putnam, commissioner of the Lighthouse Bureau, called it the most exposed site for a lighthouse in the country. "There were days when I first went on the station that I could not get away from the idea that I was the same as locked up in a cell," said William W. Williams, who spent twenty-seven years as keeper of Boon Island Light, nine miles from the nearest mainland. "When the rough weather came, seas swept the ledges clean. I was always thinking what I would do to save my life should the whole station be washed away. . . . I believe it is these things which gradually wear on the mind and finally upset the brain."

Offshore lights were by far the most demanding. Spring Point Ledge Light in Maine was surrounded by water even at low tide, and exercise was limited to a circular catwalk; fifty-six times around was a mile, one listless keeper calculated. N. A. Anderson, the first keeper at Orient Point Light in New York, spent twenty years there while his wife lived ashore on Long Island. At Colchester Reef Light on Lake Champlain in Vermont, keeper August Lorenz had to row miles to shore for supplies. One winter, he became frozen to the seat of his boat and had to chop himself free. Because of a storm, one Coast Guard keeper couldn't get to the mainland for his own wedding. When Maine's Seguin Island Light ran out of coal in the winter of 1926–27, the keeper and his wife were reduced to getting on their hands and knees to hunt for any pieces that might have fallen near the dock.

The harshest burden was by far the isolation. A poetic Coast Guardsman described his feelings in his last entry in the log at New London Ledge Light when it was deactivated in 1987. "Rock of slow torture," he wrote. "Hell on earth. . . . May New London Ledge's light shine on forever, because I'm through. I will watch it from afar while drinking a brew."

Robert T. Sterling, of Great Duck Island Light, describes the place as so lonely that when the monthly mail boat arrived with packages and letters for the keepers and their families, "it was some sport to see each one scrambling for his. At times it was like a football game, with plenty of interference. Everybody was anxious, for a letter did mean so much. Relatives and friends might be dead and buried and only the letter would tell the story." The tiny island was named for the ducks and gulls that nest there each summer. "Along about August, these gulls that have passed the summer with their young nestling about the island will all disappear," he said. "They will leave a few at a time until you will notice only a dozen or more hanging around." These, he said, were called the "old settlers," and, in a way, they are company for the isolated lighthouse keepers.

There were extraordinary daily hardships. Even though they spent cold winter nights inside the lantern rooms, the keepers weren't allowed to warm themselves for fear of steaming up the windows. Government rules prohibited supply tenders from delivering "luxuries." The only source of drinking water was often rain collected from the gutters; powdered chalk was added in a rudimentary attempt to filter out the toxic lead. Many of the frigid, windswept island lights had detached outhouses. Portland Breakwater ("Bug") Light in Maine had no keeper's house when it was first built, so its keepers had to walk 1,800 feet to work along the icy breakwater, sometimes on their hands and knees. Keeper Eldon Small spent twenty-nine years working in Maine lighthouses, but not until 1946 was he assigned to one that had electricity.

The keepers' families, of course, shared in the privations. Oscar Laighton, the son of Isles of Shoals (White Island) Light keeper Thomas Laighton, never saw a tree until he rowed to a nearby island one day when he was ten. "Not even a bayberry bush ever grew" on the island where he lived, he later recounted. On the rare occasions when they traveled to the mainland, Laighton's children called it "going to America." Colchester Reef Light keeper Walter Button kept a fruit and vegetable garden on a neighboring Lake Champlain island and sent his children off to tend it, calling them home by blowing a horn made from a conch shell. A log entry from a lighthouse off the Maine coast gives another idea of the conditions: "December 25, 1884," it says. "Could not get ashore, and consequently no Christmas presents."

In 1876, when she was fourteen, Annie Bell Hobbs, whose father was the keeper at Boon Island Light in Maine, wrote: "Out at sea, on a rock eight miles from the nearest point of land, is Boon Island, upon which I have been a prisoner, with the privilege of a yard, the past two years. After school-hours, I turn my eyes and thoughts toward the mainland and think how I should like to be there, and enjoy some of those delightful sleigh-rides which I am deprived of while shut out here from the world." The island would soon be deemed too dangerous for women and children and was restricted to men.

Poor Compensation

Some keepers made their own improvements to their lights, but they were seldom compensated. Isaac Dunham, the first keeper at Pemaquid Point Light in Maine, for instance, built a barn and house, which he sold in 1837 to his successor, Nathaniel Gamage. But when Gamage was removed in favor of a political appointee, J. P. Means, Means refused to buy the buildings. Gamage

The first keeper of Seguin Island Light, near the mouth of the Kennebec River in Maine, was a French nobleman who was appointed to the post as a reward for fighting for the American revolutionary cause. But Seguin Island, whose name comes from the Native American word for "place where the sea vomits," proved so inhospitable the count saw his house rot away in the salt air, three of his boats demolished, and his garden repeatedly flooded. So steep was the setting that later keepers were provided with Maine's only tramway, leading from the boathouse to the keeper's house.

At 186 feet above sea level, Seguin Island Light is the highest in Maine. So isolated is it that when they ran out of coal in the winter of 1926–27, the keeper and his wife were reduced to getting on their hands and knees to hunt for any pieces that might have fallen near the dock. Other keepers' wives lived on the mainland, apart from their husbands, so their children could attend school.

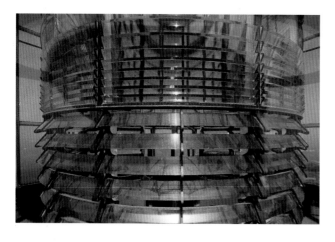

Seguin Island Light has Maine's only first-order Fresnel lens, installed in 1857 and large enough for the keeper himself to fit inside.

appealed to Treasury Secretary John Spencer but was ultimately forced to accept a paltry rent of fifteen dollars a year. When Samuel Stinson resigned as keeper of Chatham Light in Massachusetts in 1832, the notoriously stingy then-head of the lighthouse system, Stephen Pleasonton, refused to reimburse him for his house, which he had built himself. Pleasonton met his match at Baker Island Light in Maine, where the government could not prove clear title when it attempted to evict the sons of a former keeper, and they ended up getting most

of the island. At Boston Light, keeper John Hayes was nearly forced to pay out of his own pocket for the damage from a fire to the tower. The cost—216 pounds—was equal to three years salary. (Hayes's bosses ultimately let him off the hook.)

At West Quoddy Head Light in Maine, the keeper, Thomas Dextor, found the soil too sandy to grow food. He successfully appealed for a $50 raise. Ebenezer Skiff, keeper of Gay Head Light in Massachusetts, also appealed for an increase in his yearly salary of $200. When he wrote to the lighthouse office, he noted that water had to be carried from a mile away, and he was constantly cleaning the windswept soil from the glass. It was a compelling case, and Skiff got a $50 raise. He never mentioned that he was also running a profitable farm and a school on the side.

Most such entreaties fell on deaf ears. The government was unsympathetic to the conditions faced by lighthouse keepers, or their appeals for more money. As a result, many keepers moonlighted, most without permission. Ellis Dolph, who tended Whitehead Island Light in Maine, was discovered selling whale oil allocated for the lighthouse and was sacked. Tolbia Cook, keeper at Boston Light in the 1840s, set up a factory on Little Brewster Island where young girls worked in appalling conditions manufacturing cigars he fraudulently claimed were Spanish. He was eventually found out. Stanley Gunderson, keeper of Stage Harbor Light on Cape Cod, hid liquor underneath the floorboards during Prohibition. Another scandal, at Fort Pickering (Winter Island) Light in Massachusetts, revealed that the keeper had been paying someone else to do the job while he worked as the headmaster of a reform school. W. W. Wells, keeper of Saddleback Ledge Light in Maine, hoisted summer vacationers up to the tower for tours. William Brooks, keeper of Maine's Cape Neddick ("the Nubble") Light, ferried as many as 300 people a day to the lighthouse for ten cents apiece; for a nickel more, his wife would give them tours of the house. They were fired for neglecting the light. In the 1930s, tourists returned to Cape Neddick in droves to see the nineteen-pound cat that swam the channel between the lighthouse and the mainland. But it was keeper John Watts of Portland Head Light in Maine who came up with the most creative source of extra income: He charged sea captains an extra fee for blowing the fog signal.

Life on the Edge

Tragedy and sheer terror loomed omnipresent. Clinton Dalzell, keeper of Egg Rock Light in Maine, left his wife and two small children behind and set out for supplies on March 2, 1935, never to return. Before another keeper could return from shore to Saddleback Ledge Light in Maine, an unexpected storm arose that lasted twenty-one days; the keeper's fifteen-year-old son continued to light the lantern alone every night until the storm abated, and he could be relieved, nearly out of food. During a storm on January 28, 1928, so much water poured into Maine's Petit Manan Light that the keeper cut a hole in the dining room floor with an ax. Heavy seas put out the furnace, and there was no heat.

At Beavertail Light in Rhode Island, the keeper's house was swept into the sea when ice in the Providence River began to break up in March 1875, nearly killing the keeper and his son. Arthur Small, the keeper at the Palmer Island Light in Massachusetts, watched his wife drown trying to rescue him when the hurricane of 1938 washed him off the island. He made it back to the lighthouse and stayed at his post until he was found semi-conscious thirty hours later. The same hurricane swept away the keeper's house at Rhode Island's Prudence Island (Sandy Point) Light, killing the keeper's wife and son, and three guests; the keeper himself was saved when a wave swept him back to shore. The light was automated the next year, and the structures were never rebuilt. A few years later at Cleveland East Ledge Light, which sits in twenty-one feet of water two miles off the coast of Massachusetts, a hurricane blew out a glass skylight. Tons of water flooded to within two inches of shorting out the batteries as nine men frantically bailed out the engine room and stuffed the opening with mattresses.

The currents of the Connecticut River, which passed the Saybrook Breakwater Light, made it hazardous even to row ashore. In New York, Thomas A. Carroll, keeper of the Race Rock Light, dutifully attempted to row back to the lighthouse after being stranded on the mainland by a storm; he was never seen again. A huge ice floe crashed right through the kitchen of the Colchester Reef Light in Vermont, and keeper August Lorenz barely managed to retrieve his only boat from a floating cake of ice by snagging it with a long pole. A funeral for Edwin Tarr, the keeper of Long Island Head Light in Massachusetts, was held in the keeper's house during a sleet storm. Pallbearers leaving with the casket lost their footing, jumped on the coffin, and rode it like a sled to stop it from landing in the ocean.

Ice could be a very real hazard. Charles L. Knight, keeper of Hendricks Head Light in Maine, said floes of lake or river ice "are no easy job to get out of once you get in them. On each occasion when I would get caught and think my time had come, the intervention of our universe's ruler would take charge and the wind seemed to change and by a narrow squeak the shore would be made. In my opinion there is no person ever gets so close to the almighty in the time of danger as the man who follows the sea."

Some of the danger was imagined. Amos Story, the aptly named keeper of Ten Pound Island Light in Massachusetts, reported seeing a sea serpent at least fifty feet long in Gloucester Harbor. "His head appeared shaped much like the head of a sea turtle and he carried his head from ten to twelve inches above the surface of the water," Story testified. Tales of ghosts would later prompt the keeper at Minot's Light in Massachusetts to observe: "The trouble with our life here is that we have too much time to think."

Daily Life

The work itself was harder than it looked. In the mornings wicks had to be trimmed, at night heavy pails of oil carried up dozens of stairs and clockwork mechanisms wound. Reflectors had to be polished, and lenses cleaned of smoke and soot. The lantern windows also had to be washed, inside and out, rain or shine; to clean the outside, keepers balanced on the railings of the balconies. There was also continual paperwork: weather observations, records of visitors, inventories of wicks and oil, and sometimes the number and types of ships that passed. Many stations also had to be whitewashed every spring. "It is a popular idea that there is very little to do except for striking a match once a day to light the lamp," said Arthur Small, longtime keeper of the Palmer Island Light in Massachusetts. "Few of these landlubbers realize that if a fog comes in during the middle of the night, the keeper must be ready to turn on the fog signal at once, for if the fog bell is silent for a moment, even then a great vessel may be feeling her way up into the harbor, depending on the ringing of the fog signal for her safety." More duties were added with the outbreak of World War

LADIES OF THE LIGHTS: WOMEN KEEPERS

Food was running short on Matinicus Rock in January 1856. The desolate island, twenty-five miles from the nearest port of Rockland, Maine, was barren but for a lighthouse and some hens that produced a few eggs but mainly served as company for the keeper's children. Otherwise, no trees or even grass grew on the rock, which had been submerged by giant waves seven times in just the previous few months.

The government tender that delivered supplies twice a year had failed to make its regular visit to the island in September, and the keeper, Samuel Burgess, had no choice but to risk a trip ashore at the height of the winter to fetch medicine for his invalid wife and provisions for his four young daughters.

He beckoned to the oldest, Abbie, who was seventeen. Since he had been posted to the isolated light, in the deceptively mild spring of 1853, she had helped him tend the twenty-eight Argand-style lamps in the two stone towers straddling the little keeper's house. Sometimes she had even kept the light alone, when he left the island to earn extra money fishing or was delivering his catch to Rockland. "I can depend on you, Abbie," he told her as he made for the protected waters of Penobscot Bay on January 19, 1856.

Almost immediately, a storm came up. Spray crashed over the island, which was pelted with sleet and snow. Winds reached gale force. Abbie moved her mother and young sisters into one of the two light towers. At high tide, they watched as the raging seas destroyed the older of two keeper's houses. The newer house was flooded, and the water continued to rise. The noise of the tempest was so loud, it drowned out their voices. Yet Abbie ventured out to save her hens, moments before their coop was washed away.

The storm lasted for three weeks. It was another week before relief arrived. There was almost no food left. But the lights that warned ships away from the deadly ledges of the Maine coast glowed on.

"Though at times greatly exhausted by my labors, not once did the lights fail," Abbie would remember later. "Under God, I was able to perform all my accustomed duties as well as my father."

Abbie Burgess was only one of the many women who served as keepers, many of them with extraordinary bravery. Lighthouse keeping was a family affair, and wives and children often filled in for their husbands or fathers. When the men fell ill or died, or were away tending buoys or fishing, the women simply took over; they often had no choice, since there were no pensions in the lighthouse service until 1919. On his retirement at the age of seventy in 1937, keeper James W. Hinckley of Race Point Light on Cape Cod appealed for pensions to be offered to the wives of keepers, who, he said, "do just as much as the men." There was no official policy prohibiting women from working at lighthouses, and

One of the many women lighthouse keepers, Abbie Burgess kept Matinicus Rock Light lit for three weeks when her father, the keeper, was stranded ashore during a storm, rescuing her mother and young sisters in the process. She was seventeen at the time. "Under God," she said later, "I was able to perform all my accustomed duties as well as my father." (Courtesy of Jeremy D'Entremont)

women keepers seemed to become the first female federal employees by default. At least 122 women are known to have been official keepers between 1828 and 1905. Twice that number were appointed assistant keepers, and countless more served without official recognition—or pay.

The first known woman keeper was Hannah Thomas, who took over Plymouth (Gurnet) Light in Massachusetts when her husband, John, went off to fight the British during the Revolutionary War. She watched from the wooden tower as hostile British warships sailed past. Then, in 1778, the British frigate *Niger* went aground on Brown's Bank, and the crew, in a panic, hit the lighthouse with a stray shot from its cannon. When the light was later handed over to the federal government, Hannah Thomas continued as its keeper.

Like many men who had spent their lives as keepers, women keepers in the nineteenth century also faced being replaced by patronage appointees. At Old Field Point Light in New York, Mary Foster was replaced in 1869, despite petitions signed by her supporters. The community also rallied behind Angeline Nickerson, who kept Chatham Light on Cape Cod after her husband, Simeon, died in 1848; threatened with eviction in favor of a political designee, she kept the job thanks to local popular support.

Some women managed to tend lights while raising large families. Captain Ezra Daboll, the first keeper of Morgan Point Light in Connecticut, died in 1838 and was replaced by his widow, Elizabeth, who had six small children to support. One night when the light went out, she walked six miles to Groton to report it, fearful she might lose her job. "Mrs. Daboll belongs to that class of citizens whose standing in society is of the first respectability," a government evaluation read. Betsy G. Humphrey took over the light on Monhegan Island in Maine in 1862 after her husband died, watching anxiously as Confederate raiders plied the coast. With ten children to support, she remained in the job until 1880. At Owl's Head Light in Maine, Clara Emory Maddocks served as keeper for decades after her husband died, rescuing countless people and at least one cow that had fallen off a cliff.

Not all the women of the lights got such glowing reviews. When the widow of the keeper of Petit Manan Light in Maine requested the job, she was denied after an investigation found that she had let the light decline to a deplorable condition. At Stonington Harbor Light in Connecticut, where Patty Potter had succeeded her husband in 1842, an inspector reported that she "kept the most filthy house I have ever visited; everything appears to have been neglected." She was allowed to keep her job, however, until 1854.

One of the most interesting women keepers was Catherine "Kate" Moore, who took over Black Rock Harbor (Fayerweather Island) Light in Connecticut in 1871 when she was seventy-six. She had actually been doing the work since she was twelve, when she began to help her father, Captain Stephen Tomlinson Moore, whose health had failed. The 350-candlepower lamp consumed four gallons of oil each night, which she would carry up and down the stairs wearing a suit of boy's clothes. On windy nights, the light had to be tended constantly; Moore slept with her face turned toward a window so she could tell if it went out. The tower itself blew over once while she was there, on September 22, 1821. In winter, it was impossible to get to shore; in summer, she dug for oysters, tended a garden, and carved duck decoys that she sold to sportsmen. "I never had much time to get lonely," she told an interviewer after she retired at the age of eighty-four. "I had done this for so many years, and I knew no other life, so I was sort of fitted for it. I never had much of a childhood, as other children have it."

By far the most famous woman keeper was Idawalley Zorada Lewis, whose father, Captain Hosea Lewis, was the first keeper of Lime Rock Light on an island off Newport, Rhode Island. Ida Lewis was fifteen in 1857, when her family moved to the little island. After her father suffered a stroke just four months later, she nursed him, kept the light, and rowed her younger sister and brothers to school each day. Soon she could handle a boat better than anyone in New-

port, and she also was reputed to be the best swimmer. In 1858, she rescued four boys whose sailboat had capsized. In 1866, she saved three drunken soldiers who had stolen a skiff and were sinking. In 1867, she rescued three men— and the wayward sheep they had been trying to fish out of the harbor. In all, she was credited with saving up to twenty-five lives. In 1879, she was appointed keeper. By now a legend, Lewis appeared on the cover of *Harper's Weekly*, standing on a craggy shore with an angry sea behind her. The Life Saving Benevolent Association of New York sent her a silver medal. A parade was held in her honor in Newport, where she was given a mahogany rowboat with red velvet cushions, gold braid around the gunwales, and gold-plated oarlocks. President Ulysses S. Grant even came to visit, reportedly landing in ankle-deep water when he got out of his boat. "To see Ida Lewis, I'd get wet up to my armpits," Grant was reported to have said. The U.S. Life Saving Service applauded her "unquestionable nerve, presence of mind, and dashing courage."

Ida Lewis kept the light for more than fifty years. "The light is my child, and I know when it needs me, even if I sleep," she once said. When she died on October 24, 1911, all the vessels anchored in Newport Harbor tolled their bells in her memory, and in 1924, the name of the craggy island

Ida Lewis, the heroine of Lime Rock Light in Newport, Rhode Island, became nationally famous for saving as many as twenty-five lives in and around the harbor. She kept the light for more than fifty years, and it was eventually named in her honor. (Courtesy of the Library of Congress)

where she had lived was changed to Ida Lewis Rock, the only such honor ever paid a lighthouse keeper. The lighthouse, since deactivated, is now the Ida Lewis Yacht Club. A Coast Guard buoy tender was also named for her. And her successor at the lighthouse, keeper Edward Jansen, named his baby daughter Ida Lewis Jansen.

Women were not allowed to tend the cast-iron offshore "stag" lights that began to proliferate beginning in the late 1800s, and they were also seldom trained to run the coal-fired steam burners, internal combustion engines, and electrical equipment that began to be used for fog signals and lights. A few women returned to lighthouse duty when the Coast Guard began allowing female enlistment in 1973.

As for Abbie Burgess, her father lost his job as keeper at Matinicus Rock to a Republican appointee in 1860. But she stayed behind to help and, at twenty-two, married the new keeper's son, Isaac H. Grant, who later took over as keeper himself; she was finally officially appointed assistant keeper. The couple had four children on the inhospitable spit of rock, one of whom died as an infant and is buried there. In 1872, they were transferred to Whitehead Island Light in Maine. They resigned in 1890, and she died two years later.

"Sometimes I think the time is not far distant when I shall climb these lighthouse stairs no more," she wrote in the quiet of her old age. "It has almost seemed to me that the light was part of myself. I wonder if the care of the lighthouse will follow my soul after it has left this worn-out body!" If she ever had a gravestone, Abbie wrote, she wanted it to be carved in the shape of a lighthouse or beacon.

In 1945, the historian Edward Rowe Snow placed a tiny lighthouse on the grave of Abbie Burgess Grant.

So isolated is Seguin Island Light, the wife of one keeper kept playing the same piece of music over and over on a player piano her husband had bought to keep her entertained. Finally driven mad by the redundant tune, he strangled her and took an ax to the piano. Later keepers reporting hearing a phantom piano playing.

Connecticut's Five Mile Point Light was built on the spot where a farmer named Amos Morris outwitted a British landing party one night during the Revolutionary War by mounting his horse and calling out orders to the rocks and trees as though they were defending troops. When the lighthouse was constructed later, he was made the keeper—though he quit after only three weeks.

Abbie Burgess Grant spent so much of her life in lighthouses, she once wrote that she wanted her gravestone carved in the shape of a lighthouse or beacon. Her wish was answered in 1945, when the historian Edward Rowe Snow placed a tiny lighthouse on her grave.

II, when the government began installing telephones in most of the offshore light stations so the keepers could watch out for German submarines.

A Lighthouse Bureau machinist, Fred Morong of Lubec, Maine, wrote a poem about what he considered the worst job: polishing the brasswork. It read, in part:

"O, what is the bane of a lighthouse keeper's life,
That causes him worry, struggle and strife,
That makes him use cuss words, and beat at his wife?
It's brasswork . . .

The devil himself could never invent
A material causing more world-wide lament,
And in Uncle Sam's service about 90 percent
Is brasswork.

But not all was drudgery and gloom. Captain William Long, keeper of Boston Light in the 1850s, had a daughter named Lucy who was popular with the local harbor pilots. One of them, Albert Small, proposed to her in the lighthouse tower, and they were married on June 16, 1853. Cape Neddick ("the Nubble") Light in Maine hosted no fewer than three weddings, one of them of a keeper's daughter who was married in the lantern room.

Great Duck Island in Maine boasted its own schoolhouse, thanks to the arrival in 1902 of an assistant keeper, Nathan Adam Reed, who had sixteen children. Reed's arrival immediately doubled the number of potential students, and the island got its own one-room schoolhouse and a teacher in 1904. Usually, education was a major problem. The wives of the keepers on Seguin Island lived on the mainland, apart from their husbands, so their children could attend school. David Winchester, keeper of Cape Neddick ("the Nubble") Light, put his six-year-old son, Rickie, in a wooden box each morning and launched him on a cable fifty feet above the water across the channel to the mainland. When the Coast Guard discovered it, they put an end to this mode of transportation.

Several lights were tended by the same families for generations. Milton Reamy, for example, served as keeper of lonely Minot's Ledge Light from 1887 to 1915, followed by his son, who stayed until 1924. Wolcott Marr was born, married, and died at Hendricks Head Light, which he had taken over from his keeper father. Captain Joshua Strout tended Portland Head Light for fifty years after retiring from the sea in 1866. His wife, Mary, was assistant keeper; their son, Joseph, succeeded them, serving until 1928.

Heroes in the Storm

Rescues broke up the routine of lighthouse life. Fred Bohm, keeper of Duxbury Pier ("Bug") Light in Massachusetts, was credited with saving ninety people, including thirty-six Girl Scouts, in one year. William Howard, keeper of Wing's Neck Light in Massachusetts, was said to have rescued thirty-seven people. Marcus Hanna, while keeper of Cape Elizabeth Light in Maine, was awarded the Gold Life Saving Medal, the highest civilian award for lifesaving, for rescuing sailors from the wrecked schooner *Australia* in 1885. Oliver Brooks, who tended Faulkners Island Light in Connecticut, responded to seventy-one shipwrecks in thirty-one years.

Rescues worked both ways. Residents in dories fought a midwinter gale to deliver a doctor to Egg Rock Light in Massachusetts when the keeper, Thomas Widger, signaled that a member of his family was gravely ill. At Bird Island Light in Massachusetts, the keeper extinguished the light intentionally to signal for a doctor to come and help his child, dying of pneumonia. Help did come, but too late. This was often the case, if help came at all. Two of Faulkners Island keeper Arthur Jensen's children died as infants at the lonely Connecticut lighthouse where medical attention was unavailable. The pregnant wife of Joseph Muse, the keeper of Maine's Baker Island Light, went into labor in a gale. She was picked up by the Coast Guard, but delivered while still two miles out to sea. Colchester Reef, Vermont, keeper Walter Button rang the fog bell to summon a doctor when his wife went into labor. Attempting to respond, the doctor was carried miles off course by ice floes. The baby was born unassisted.

Military Significance

The strategic importance and coastal location of the lights also made them military targets. Boston Light was taken by the British occupying Boston Harbor at the outset of the Revolutionary War until, in July 1775, a small band of Americans landed there, removed the lantern, and set fire to the lighthouse. The British immediately began repairs and posted extra guards. A second raiding party of 300 Continental soldiers succeeded in disabling the light again a few weeks later but was stranded when the tide went out. British reinforcements headed for the island, and the Battle of Boston Light looked lost until a cannon shot fired from Nantasket scored a direct hit on a British boat, throwing the Redcoats into disarray. Only one American was lost, compared to heavy English casualties. When the British were

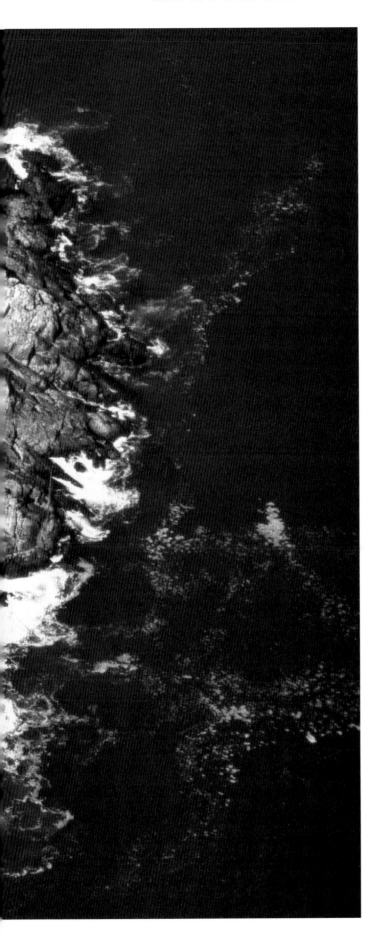

Built on a desolate exposed rock, Saddleback Ledge Light in Maine was so inhospitable that soil had to be brought there from the mainland in burlap bags to grow vegetables. Most of the time, it was washed away. The only way to get on and off the ledge was on a bosun's chair connected to a hoist and boom, since high seas normally submerged the landing area—and, occasionally, the keeper's quarters.

forced to lift their siege for good on June 13, 1776, they blew up the lighthouse themselves. It was not rebuilt until 1783. The British also burned Beavertail Light in Rhode Island when they abandoned Newport Harbor in 1779; the stone tower survived but the rest was not rebuilt until 1790. Plymouth (Gurnet) Light in Massachusetts also was a target, so residents of Plymouth, Duxbury, and Kingston built a crude fort to protect it. When the British frigate *Niger* went aground on nearby shoals in 1778, a shot from the ship pierced the wall of the lighthouse.

Lighthouses saw more action in the War of 1812. Boston Light keeper Jonathan Bruce watched from his tower as the USS *Chesapeake* fought the English warship *Shannon* on June 1, 1813. "Tell the men to fire faster and not to give up the ship," the *Chesapeake's* wounded captain, James Lawrence, said from the deck. "Fight her till she sinks." But both Lawrence and the *Chesapeake* succumbed. The Bakers Island, Massachusetts, keeper took a more direct role when he saw the USS *Constitution* trying to evade the British warships *Tenedos* and *Endymion*. The keeper, Joseph Perkins, rowed to *Old Ironsides* and piloted her into Salem Harbor, where the British dared not follow. And at Scituate Light in Massachusetts, the two young daughters of keeper Simeon Bates frightened off a British raiding party on September 1, 1814, by picking up a fife and drum and playing marching tunes with all their might. The British turned and retreated to their ship, the man-of-war *La Hogue*, after mistaking nineteen-year-old Rebecca and fourteen-year-old Abigail Bates for a militia unit. Rebecca Bates's famous fife is in the town historical museum. British marauders also stole American lighthouse apparatus in the War of 1812 and took it to Bermuda, where some of it was bought by American privateers and sold back to the U.S. government.

Improved Conditions

Conditions finally began to improve for keepers with the creation of the U.S. Lighthouse Board in 1852. Made up of military officers, engineers, and scientists, the Lighthouse Board immediately started to replace deteriorating lighthouse structures and equipment. Keepers began undergoing training for the first time. In 1876, portable libraries of sixty books in large oak crates began to be circulated among light stations. Uniforms were introduced in 1884 for male keepers: doublebreasted coats with brass buttons and caps with yellow lighthouse badges just above the visor. In 1896, President Grover Cleveland ended patronage appointments, placing keepers under the Civil Service Act. Written and verbal examinations would thereafter be required, and a merit system was used for assignments and promotions.

Supply ships also made more reliable visits. But with them came a new source of anxiety for keepers: inspectors newly assigned to every lighthouse district. Keepers constantly dreaded these inspections. Captain Edward Carpender, inspector of lighthouses in the Northeast, told of how he surprised the keeper at Highland (Cape Cod) Light trying to "make a hasty rub-up" in anticipation of his visit.

There was nothing feared more, however, than letting the lantern go dark. The keeper of Newburyport Harbor (Plum Island) Light in Massachusetts was caught unexpectedly in a gale and was unable to reach the tower and illuminate the beacon. That night, the brig *Richmond Packet* struck the rocks and broke up, and the captain's wife drowned. "Surely the lighthouse keeper has a responsible office," Henry David Thoreau observed. "When his lamp goes out, he goes out; or, at most, only one such accident is pardoned."

Maine's Boon Island is one of the nation's most barren lighthouse sites. One keeper compared living there to being "locked up in a cell. I was always thinking what I would do to save my life should the whole station be washed away. . . . I believe it is these things which gradually wear on the mind and finally upset the brain."

Pemaquid Point Light has been automated since 1934. The keeper's house is now a fishermen's museum with the original 1855 fourth-order Fresnel lens from Baker Island Light, along with charts, buoys, nets, hooks, measuring tools, and the shell of a twenty-eight-pound lobster.

Some keepers made their own improvements to their lights, though they were seldom compensated. Isaac Dunham, the first keeper at Pemaquid Point Light in Maine, for instance, built a barn and house. But later keepers refused to pay for the buildings when they inherited the lighthouse.

The Flying Santa

One of the New England lighthouse rescues with the longest-lasting impact wasn't of a ship, but of an airplane.

It was a few days before Christmas in 1929 when pilot William Wincapaw shrugged off reports of snow and took off in his single-engine plane above the rocky coast of Maine. It wasn't the first time Wincapaw, a tough Maine native and experienced flyer, chanced a trip in heavy weather. But it would nearly be the last.

Soon Wincapaw had flown into a raging snowstorm, and even he was outmatched. So much snow was falling that he couldn't see out the window. The situation grew more desperate by the minute. His instruments weren't working properly, and he had been blown miles off course by heavy winds. He was flying blind, and he was almost out of fuel.

Wincapaw chanced a quick descent below the clouds, hoping to break free of the weather. That's when an unexpected but familiar light pierced the sheets of falling snow: the beam from Dice Head Light in Castine. The beams of five more lighthouses led him safely home to Rockland.

A grateful Wincapaw took off again a few days later and dropped Christmas packages with cookies, coffee, tea, a copy of the *Farmer's Almanac*, and notes of thanks to each of the lighthouse keepers and their families. The gifts became an annual tradition. A coffee company loaned Wincapaw a sea plane, and soon other businesses and individuals were contributing cash and gifts. Keepers' children collected rocks and branches to spell out "Hi, Santa," or "Merry Christmas" in the snow. Wincapaw became immortalized as the Flying Santa.

Wincapaw faced myriad difficulties. At Minot's Ledge Light, for example, which stands in the open ocean, he had to tie two or three packages together with rope so they would snare on one of the upper platforms of the tower.

In 1936, when Wincapaw left for Bolivia and a job flying gold from mountain mines, the writer and historian Edward Rowe Snow took over. Snow liked to tell the story of his late arrival at one lighthouse in Massachusetts at Christmas 1939. "The hour was approaching when the plane should make its appearance, so the keeper called out to his wife, 'Has Santa arrived yet, dear?'" he remembered. "Before the lady could reply, there was a terrific crash upstairs and the Christmas bundle came hurtling along the upper hall after its surprising entrance through a skylight. His wife was equal to the occasion. She answered, without a tremor in her voice: 'Yes, dear. We can start the party now.'"

After Wincapaw returned from South America, he and Snow flew the Santa missions together until 1947, when Wincapaw had a heart attack while flying his plane and died when it crashed into Rockland Harbor. Hundreds attended

William Wincapaw credited the lighthouses with saving his life while he was flying in a storm and returned the favor by delivering gifts and food each Christmas to the lonely keepers and their families. (Courtesy of Jeremy D'Entremont. Reprinted by permission of William Wincapaw III.)

his funeral service, and lighthouses all over New England sounded their foghorns in his honor.

Snow continued the custom until 1981, when he suffered a stroke and passed on his Santa suit to the Hull Life-saving Museum, which enlisted volunteers to take over the role without interruption. By then, a helicopter was used. There were still a few resident caretakers, but most of the presents went to Coast Guard personnel and their families. Drops were made at thirty-one lighthouses and Coast Guard stations from Maine to New York. Businesses continued to donate gifts and helicopter time.

In 1998, the Friends of Flying Santa was incorporated, just in time for the tradition to reach its seventieth anniversary. It found no shortage of new volunteers to don the worn red Santa suit.

Like many Northeast lighthouses, Pemaquid Point Light is often shrouded by thick fog.

Living at a lighthouse meant constant privation. The pregnant wife of the keeper of Maine's Baker Island Light, for example, went into labor in a gale and delivered while still two miles out to sea after being picked up by the Coast Guard. The lighthouse was automated in 1966 and has twice survived announced plans by the Coast Guard to deactivate it, thanks to a spirited defense in its support by mariners and neighbors.

Above: *Keeping a lighthouse meant more than simply turning on the beacon every night. During the day, wicks had to be trimmed, and oil carried up dozens of stairs. One of the most time-consuming duties was cleaning the delicate Fresnel lenses, such as this first-order lens from Gay Head Light in Martha's Vineyard, now in the Martha's Vineyard Historical Museum. Pleading poverty, Gay Head keeper Ebenezer Skiff appealed for an increase in his salary for doing all this work. He never mentioned that he was also running a profitable farm and a school on the side.*

Left: *Another hazard of lighthouse work was cleaning the lantern windows, rain or shine. To clean the outside, keepers balanced on the railings of the balconies, even 180 feet up as at Fire Island Light in New York.*

CHAPTER 4

Legends of the Lights:

Madness, Murder, Shipwrecks, Ghosts, and Pirates

Facing page: So quintessential a New England lighthouse is Maine's Marshall Point Light, it was used by the makers of the movie Forrest Gump as the ending point of the title character's fictional cross-country run. Built in 1857 to mark the entrance to Port Clyde, the lighthouse is now owned by the town and houses the Marshall Point Lighthouse Museum.

Above: Ned's Point Light in southeastern Massachusetts has helped guide vessels into Mattapoisett Harbor since 1837; with the exception of modifications to the lantern room to accommodate a larger lens, it looks much as it did when it was built. When the light was automated in 1923, however, the keeper's house was moved on a barge across Buzzard's Bay to Wing's Neck Light in Bourne.

Marcus Hanna received the Congressional Medal of Honor for his heroism in the Civil War. That alone made him particularly distinguished among the ranks of U.S. lighthouse keepers. But not even war prepared him for the harrowing events of January 28, 1885, at Cape Elizabeth Light in Maine.

Despite suffering from a bad cold, Hanna had already stayed up all night sounding the steam-powered fog whistle into the darkness of a blizzard he described as "one of the coldest and most violent storms of snow, wind and vapor I have ever witnessed." Finally, at 6 A.M., he was replaced by the assistant keeper, Hiram Staples. After his wife promised to put out the lights at sunrise, Hanna dragged himself to bed, exhausted.

The lives of all the people at the lighthouse were about to change forever.

At 8:40 A.M., the veil of fog and snow was punctured by a set of ship's masts, leaning at a precarious tilt. They belonged to the schooner Australia out of Boothbay, Maine, aground on Dyer's Ledge and weighted down with a cargo including 150 barrels of mackerel meant for Boston. Two crewmen, Irving Pierce and William Kellar, clung desperately to the icy rigging; the captain had been swept away.

Awakened, Hanna struggled through the massive snowdrifts to the shore, only to find that the survivors were by now nearly frozen alive in temperatures of ten degrees below zero. "I felt a terrible responsibility thrust upon me, and I resolved to attempt the rescue at any hazard," he remembered later. But the door to the building where the rescue boat was kept was blocked with snow. Hanna tried to throw a line, but the wind was too strong. Nearly frozen himself, he waded up to his waist into the numbing cold of the Atlantic. This time, when he threw his line, Pierce managed to catch it. Hanna pulled the man to shore, across the waves and rocks. "He was totally blind from exposure to the cold, and the expression of his face I shall not soon forget," he said. His strength failing, Hanna somehow tossed the line to Kellar after several tries. Staples and two neighbors arrived then and carried the sailors to safety. Their frozen clothes had to be cut from their bodies. When they could talk again, they said they owed their lives to Marcus Hanna.

Hanna received the Gold Life Saving Medal for his heroism, the highest such civilian award, and in 1997, a Coast Guard buoy tender was named for him. But it was not the only shipwreck story at the lights, which also had more than their share of dramas involving ghosts, pirates, murders, madness, and mysteries.

Shipwrecks

Many of the wrecks, of course, preceded the construction of the lights, helping make the case for them in the first place. The transatlantic steamer California went aground at Ram Island Ledge near Portland, Maine, in a snowstorm on February 24, 1900, for instance. And while the passengers and crew were rescued, the near-catastrophe showed the need for a lighthouse at Ram Island Ledge. Eight ships were lost in eight years before the government approved building Race Rock Light off Long Island. In one of the worst, the Atlantic, sailing from New York to Boston on November 26, 1846, was disabled when a steam pipe burst. The vessel dropped anchor, but a gale dragged her toward the shoals, where she broke apart. Only fourteen of the fifty-nine aboard survived. Several other people who had tickets for the voyage, including Senator Daniel Webster, had refused to embark in New York because of the threatening weather.

The Nottingham Galley, bound for Boston from London, struck Boon Island off the Maine coast on December 11, 1710. The ship and its cargo of butter and cheese were lost, and, while all hands got ashore, there was nothing to eat on the barren island. When one person died, the rest finally resorted to cannibalism. The crew was rescued after twenty-four days. When the story leaked out, the captain, John Deane, was forced to disappear into the Russian naval service, though he later re-emerged as an English diplomat and spy. A lighthouse was later built on the dangerous rock, though even it was washed away twice by storms.

In many places, wrecks continued even after lighthouses were in operation. Sixty ships were lost in a single storm near New York's Eatons Neck Light on December 23, 1811, for example. The steamship Lexington burned off Eatons Neck on January 3, 1849, killing 130 passengers and crew. On November 3, 1861, the square-rigger Maritana bound for Boston from Liverpool crashed into Shag Rocks in Boston Harbor; bodies of the crew washed up right under Boston Light and were buried on Little Brewster Island. In 1872, the steamer Metis was rammed by the schooner Mattie Cushing near Watch Hill Light in Rhode Island, killing twenty people; thirty-three others were rescued. In one of the worst marine disasters in New England history, the coastal passenger steamer City of Columbus ran aground near Gay Head Light on Martha's Vineyard January 19, 1884.

Keeper Horace N. Pease saved a few lives, but at least 100 passengers and crew died of the cold or drowned within twenty minutes. On September 16, 1903, the fishing schooner *George F. Edmunds* crashed on the rocky shore near Pemaquid Point Light in Maine when the captain overshot his course by 800 yards in thick fog and gale-force winds. He and thirteen members of his crew were killed; two survived.

Some of these wrecks occurred beneath the very beacons of the lighthouse towers. John Bragg Downs, who tended New Hampshire's Isles of Shoals (White Island) Light, was alone with a friend in his kitchen during a snowstorm one night in the early 1830s. "Well, John, what would you think if somebody was to knock at the door just now," the friend said as a joke. "I should think it must be the devil himself," Downs replied, "for no human being could land on White Island this night and live." Just then they heard a knock above the howling wind. The two men looked at each other fearfully before they gathered up the courage to open the door. It was a sailor, beaten and bleeding, who told them that a Russian brig had hit the rocks. Together, they rescued the entire crew of fourteen. In 1962 at Watch Hill Light, the crewman on watch knocked on the door and calmly told the keeper there was a ship in his front yard: the 3,200-ton *Leif Viking*, which had landed on the rocks. It took nine days to dislodge, when it was towed off for repairs.

The *Abbie B. Cramer*, a three-masted schooner with a cargo of coal, went ashore 150 yards from Annisquam Harbor Light in Massachusetts in a nor'easter in September 1890. Crewmembers took to the rigging and eventually were rescued. Local residents heated their homes with salvaged coal all winter. At least eleven ships were wrecked in the vicinity of Maine's Owl's Head Light between 1873 and 1896. Two hit the rocks on November 30, 1842, alone. All aboard were saved by the keeper, Perley Haines. And in 1852 at Highland (Cape Cod) Light, the bark *Josepha* struck a sandbar half a mile from the lighthouse in a thick fog. "I was almost the first one down on the shore opposite the wreck," the keeper, Enoch Hamilton, later remembered. Two would-be rescuers drowned in the heavy seas while trying to reach the ship in a rowboat, and fourteen of the sixteen members of the crew also perished. One of the survivors, John Jasper, later became the captain of a transatlantic liner and ordered that the flag be dipped in salute whenever he passed Highland Light.

On Christmas Eve 1886, the Portland, Maine, po-

Cape Elizabeth Light in Maine was the site of the heroic rescue by keeper Marcus Hanna of two crewmen frozen to the rigging of their ship, which had crashed into the rocky coastline in a monumental snowstorm. Hanna nearly froze to death himself while wading up to his waist in the numbing cold of the Atlantic.

lice chief asked Portland Head Light keeper Joshua Strout to keep an eye out for a ship called the *Annie C. Maguire*; the owner was in deep financial trouble, and its creditors had ordered that the ship be seized. Because of that, and since it was headed to Quebec from Buenos Aires, Stout didn't think the ship was likely to appear in Casco Bay. But that night, as a heavy snow fell, there was a sudden crash; it was the *Annie C. Maguire*, which had lost her bearings and was stranded on the rocks just yards from Strout's front door. Quick action saved all eighteen aboard, but the debt still needed to be resolved. When the ship was scoured, no money or documents were found. The captain's wife, it turns out, had stashed them in a hatbox, which she carried with her from the vessel.

Also near Portland Head Light, the steamer *Bohemian* bound for America from Liverpool with 218 immigrants and crew hit Alden's Rock on February 22, 1864, in heavy snow and fog. In the scramble to escape, the Number Two lifeboat broke from its hoist, and forty

Lighthouses helped reduce the number of shipwrecks, but couldn't altogether prevent them. Sixty ships were lost in a single storm near New York's Eatons Neck Light, for instance. In 1849, Eatons Neck became the site of the first lifesaving station built by the federal government; the buildings now are used as housing for U.S. Coast Guard personnel.

people dropped to their deaths in the sea.

In a tragedy that moved all of New England, the *Pocahontas* bound for Newburyport was wrecked in 1839 on a sandbar near Newburyport Harbor (Plum Island) Light in Massachusetts; all lives were lost. The same year, the brig *Richmond Packet*, also bound for Newburyport with a cargo of flour and corn, was driven by a gale into the rocks one night. The lighthouse on Plum Island was dark at the time because the keeper had been stranded on the mainland by the storm. While the crew survived, the captain's wife was swept away.

On the night of January 21, 1941, the fishing schooner *Mary E. O'Hara* struck an anchored and unlighted barge in Boston Harbor just after passing Graves Light. Crew members held on to the rigging, but only five were still alive when help arrived at dawn. Also at Graves Light, the 419-foot freighter *City of Salisbury*, carrying a cargo of zoo animals, struck a reef in 1938. Humans and animals alike were all saved.

On November 17, 1984, the 85-foot tugboat *Celtic* towing a 140-foot barge passed Connecticut's Sheffield Island (Norwalk) Light and promptly disappeared with all six crewmen. There was no distress call, and searchers found no trace of either vessel. Finally, divers discovered the *Celtic* upright on her keel on the sea floor with the sunken barge nearby. But there was still no easy answer to the mystery of why they went down. One explanation is that the barge's cargo shifted suddenly, taking both craft to the bottom instantly.

Stranger Than Life

A number of wrecks had eerie overtones. The brig *Maine*, bound for New Orleans on her maiden voyage with a crew of nine, for example, passed under Owl's Head Light on November 9, 1844, never to be seen again. Three years later, another ship arrived carrying the *Maine*'s atlas, charts, and mahogany sea chest. When questioned, the crew said the items had been brought aboard by three Portuguese sailors who then jumped ship, leaving them behind. The mystery was never solved.

On December 22, 1850, a gale crushed a coastal schooner up against the rocks at Owl's Head. The schooner had been anchored in the harbor, and only three people were aboard that night: the first mate, Richard Ingraham; his fiancee, Lydia Dyer; and a deckhand, Roger Elliott. As the ship began to break apart, they huddled together under blankets against the snow and spray. Finally, Elliott made a desperate dash for help, somehow struggling across the ice-covered rocks to the lighthouse; within a few days, he would die of exposure. The keeper, William Masters, gathered a rescue party and found Ingraham and Dyer in a block of ice, which they dragged back to the lighthouse. There the couple was carefully thawed out in tubs of water. They recovered, married, and had four children, though Ingraham never went to sea again.

On November 28, 1842, seaman Thomas King of the bark *Isidore*, which was about to sail from York, Maine, had a dream in which the ship was lost. The next night, another sailor on the vessel dreamed of seeing seven coffins on the shore—one of them his own. King begged Captain Ileander Foss to go without him. Foss refused, reminding King that he had signed a contract. News of the premonitions had by then swept town, and women at the wharf were sobbing as the *Isidore* faded from their view and sailed past Cape Neddick ("the Nubble") Light. Within hours, the wreckage of a ship began to wash up on shore, including seven bodies—one of them the sailor who had dreamed of seven coffins. The *Isidore* had sunk. But Thomas King was not among the victims; he had hidden in the woods as the ship left York. Fishermen later spoke of seeing a ghostly bark with a crew that stood staring straight ahead—every man dripping wet.

When a schooner went down near Maine's Mount Desert Rock Light in the 1880s, a sailor clinging to a capsized lifeboat saw a bundle made of oilskin. Inside he found a baby, which he cradled to his chest until the two were rescued. At Hendricks Head Light in Maine, a

Even after a powerful first-order Fresnel lens was installed in Gay Head Light on Martha's Vineyard, the so-called Devil's Ledge it overlooks claimed many ships. In one of New England's worst maritime disasters, the passenger steamer City of Columbus was wrecked there on January 19, 1884, and about 100 passengers and crew were drowned. Lighthouse keeper Horace Pease was credited with rescuing some of the survivors, at great risk to his own life. (Courtesy of Jeremy D'Entremont)

March gale purportedly crushed a ship against the rocks. The keeper and his wife could see survivors clinging to the rigging in the freezing spray, but there was no way to reach them through the ten-foot seas. They built a bonfire as a signal that the wreck had been spotted and waited until a rescue could be attempted. Soon they noticed a bundle bobbing toward them in the surf. It was two feather mattresses, cushioning a box. Inside, a baby girl, alive and crying, with a message from the child's mother commending her to God. By then, the vessel had been pulled beneath the waves with all hands. The keeper and his wife, the story goes, adopted the orphaned infant.

The story of the Hendricks Head Light baby has been widely discredited by historians. And it is true that certain lighthouse lore has been exaggerated. Keeper Joseph Maddocks of Owl's Head Light was said to have seen a fisherman offshore one night, hauling in his nets. The next day, the boat was in the same spot—with no one aboard. Maddocks rowed out to the trawler, where he noticed a line leading to the water. He pulled it up—and with it, the fisherman's body. Another version puts the story at Mount Desert Rock Light. In this telling, the fisherman was pulled overboard by a hundred-pound halibut.

Plenty of strange tales, however, have never been explained. Long Island Head Light is said to be haunted by the Woman in Scarlet, the ghost of a widow whose husband was a British soldier buried on the island near the outset of the Revolutionary War. The keepers at Boon Island Light have seen the ghost of a sad-faced young woman in white, alternately said to have been the mistress of the captain of the *Nottingham Galley* or the young widow of a keeper who died one winter at the lighthouse. Keepers assigned to Sankaty Head Light on Nantucket reported strange events, including pots and pans that flew around the kitchen. And at Minot's Ledge Light in Massachusetts, keepers saw doors open and close

In 1962, the keeper at Watch Hill Light in Rhode Island was summoned to the door by a knock. A sailor calmly told him that the 3,200-ton Leif Viking had come ashore in the front yard of the lighthouse. It took nine days to dislodge.

by themselves and heard a tapping on the walls—a signal system once used by Joseph Antoine and Joseph
Wilson, the assistant keepers killed when the first cast-
iron lighthouse on the site was demolished in a storm.
One Minot's Ledge Light keeper complimented his assistant on how well he had shined the lantern, only to
be told that the assistant hadn't done it. Passing sailors
swear they've seen a figure clinging to the ladder, dripping wet, and shouting "Keep away! Keep away!" in Portuguese—Antoine's native tongue.

One of the earliest such stories occurred off Rhode
Island's Block Island, an area of deadly shoals known as
the Graveyard of the Atlantic. Before the island got its
lighthouses, locals would build signal fires on the shoreline—not to warn ships, but to lure them to the rocks,
where their valuable cargoes could be salvaged. One
stormy December night in the late 1700s, the Dutch
ship *Palatine*, carrying wealthy Dutch and German settlers to Philadelphia, was wrecked this way. But when
the islanders had trapped it on the reefs, they found the
passengers were starving and the crew was gone—mutinied, it turned out, after storms delayed the voyage and
the food ran out. The captain had been murdered and
the passengers left to their fate. Their sympathies aroused,
the residents rescued the survivors, set the ship afire, and
pushed it back to sea, only to hear screams from the hold.
A woman passenger had hidden herself and was beyond
help on the burning ship.

Soon there were reports of "a great irradiance" north
of Block Island, taking the form of a flaming ship, and
the sound of a woman screaming. "I was so distressed by
the sight that we followed the burning ship to its watery
grave, but failed to find survivors and flotsam," recounted
the captain of the English trader *Somerset*. Scientists have
tried to explain what has since become known as the
Palatine Light, speculating that it might be gas escaping
from the ocean floor, or schools of reflective fish. But
when the fog is thick, sailors say they see the *Palatine*
and hear the hapless woman screaming in its ghostly
hold.

At Penfield Reef Light in Connecticut in 1916,
keeper Fred Jordan was so determined to begin his leave
on Christmas Eve as scheduled that he set out in a rowboat in a storm. In his haste, he also wrote a note to his
assistant keeper asking that the logbook be brought up
to date. Jordan capsized and drowned, the note still ab-
sentmindedly stuck in the pocket of the white suit he
was wearing. The assistant keeper, who succeeded Jor-

The Annie C. Maguire *ran aground at Portland Head Light
in Maine on Christmas Eve 1886. Quick action by lighthouse
keeper Joshua Strout saved all eighteen aboard. The boat had
been ordered seized by its creditors for nonpayment of debt, but
the captain's wife managed to hide the documents and money
in a hatbox. (Courtesy of Jeremy D'Entremont)*

*Graves Light in Boston Harbor was the scene of the
wreck of the fishing schooner* Mary E. O'Hara, *which
struck an anchored and unlighted barge one night. Crew
members held on to the rigging, but only five were still
alive when help arrived at dawn. Contrary to conjec-
ture, the lighthouse is not called "Graves" because of
its deadly location, however. It was named for a colonial captain, Thomas Graves.*

dan, later told of seeing the figure of a man dressed in white descending the stairway of the tower and disappearing into the darkness outside the lighthouse, which sits alone in the ocean on a pier; he also found the logbook opened to the page that Jordan was so anxious be brought up to date. In later years, a yacht in distress was piloted into the harbor by a man who suddenly appeared in a rowboat, then just as suddenly vanished. A mysterious man was credited with saving two boys when their boat capsized, pulling them to safety at the lighthouse; when they went inside to thank him, there was no one there. Mariners still report seeing a figure in the lantern room of the lighthouse, which now is automated and unstaffed.

When John "Ernie" Randolph, the keeper of New London Ledge Light in Connecticut, discovered in 1936 that his wife had run off with a Block Island ferry captain, he slit his own throat and jumped to his death from the steel door of the lantern tower to the rocks four stories below. Later keepers said they saw the steel door, which was bolted from the inside, open by itself. "The wind can be blamed for many of the strange noises we hear, but I know the sound of that door opening up, and no wind ever did that," one uneasy witness said. Later residents heard footsteps or felt cold spots in the lighthouse. Ernie is also blamed for mischievously switching the fog signal on and off and for untying boats to float off with the current.

What's in a Name?

Mystery? Intrigue? Not surprising, considering that even the places where the lights were built have melodramatic histories. Highland (Cape Cod) Light is in the town of Truro, originally known as Dangerfield. "This was a very appropriate name, for I afterward read on a monument in the graveyard the following inscription: Sacred to the memory of fifty-seven citizens who were lost in seven vessels which foundered at sea," Henry David Thoreau observed on a visit. The spit of land for which Thacher Island (Cape Ann) Lights is named was given to Anthony

The vicinity of Owl's Head Light in Maine is a notorious place for shipwrecks. At least eleven ships were wrecked there in one twenty-three-year period—two of them on the same night. In one epic mystery, the brig Maine left port and passed under Owl's Head Light in 1844, never to be seen again; three years later, another ship arrived carrying the Maine's atlas, charts, and mahogany sea chest. In 1850, rescuers found three people frozen solid on their sinking ship in a gale. Two of them, a man and a woman, survived and were later married.

Boon Island Light off the Maine coast. This rocky spit has been the scene of shipwrecks and cannibalism before a lighthouse was built here, and still more shipwrecks since. One keeper fell ill and died almost immediately after taking the job, leaving his young wife alone with his body on the barren island. Fisherman found her there, wandering outside, completely insane. (Courtesy of the Library of Congress)

Thacher in 1635 as compensation after all five of his children drowned in front of his eyes in a shipwreck as they were making the journey by sea from Ipswich to Marblehead.

The danger of the coast is evident in many of the names that sailors gave it. In addition to the Graveyard of the Atlantic, mariners have called the area around Block Island the Stumbling Block. Long Island Sound was known in colonial times as the Devil's Belt. According to Native American legend, the evil spirit Habbamoko was pushed back across Long Island Sound to Throg's Neck, making his escape by tossing huge stones into the water and stepping across them to Long Island. The waters there were dubbed the Devil's Stepping Stones, later shortened to Stepping Stones, the site of Stepping Stones Light. Cape Neddick ("the Nubble") Light in Maine sits on an island of weird rock formations once known as the Devil's Oven. New York's Horton Point, the site of Horton Point Light, was nicknamed Dead Man's Cove.

There are two explanations for the name of Boon Island, where Boon Island Light was built. The first says it derived its name from a boon, or barrel of emergency provisions, left on the barren island for shipwrecked sailors after survivors from the *Nottingham Galley* were forced to resort to cannibalism. The second dates to 1682, when the crew of a coastal trader, the *Increase*, was rescued after managing to build a signal fire. So grateful were they, this story goes, they considered their deliverance a boon from God.

The derivation of the name of Point Judith in Rhode Island is also in dispute. It may have been named for the biblical Tribe of Judah or for the mother-in-law of a wealthy local merchant. The best explanation is that the daughter of a sea captain, on a ship lost in fog before there was a lighthouse at the site, was the first to spot land. The captain still couldn't make it out, however. "Point, Judy. Point!" he shouted.

Other lighthouse names have more mundane beginnings. Cleveland East Ledge Light in Massachusetts marks an area named for President Grover Cleveland, whose Summer White House was in nearby Buzzards Bay. Hospital Point Light in Massachusetts is on the site of a former smallpox hospital. Ten Pound Island Light, also in Massachusetts, commemorates the amount of money settlers paid the Native Americans for it. Isle Au Haut (Robinson Point) Light in Maine is on an island named by the French explorer Samuel Champlain, who was impressed by its great height. Maine's Owl's Head Light is on a promontory where two hollows in a rocky cliff appear as owl's eyes, and the ridge between them as the beak. And the site of Great Captain Island Light in Connecticut was named by Captain Daniel Patrick as a tribute—to himself.

Some of the more obvious-sounding lighthouse names are actually among the oddest. Sands Point Light in New York is named not because the land was sandy, but for Captain John Sands, the captain of a coastal schooner. Graves Light in Boston Harbor is also named for a colonial captain, Thomas Graves.

One of the most extraordinary histories occurred at New York's Execution Rocks, which was used by the

Above: The area near Block Island North Light has been called the "Graveyard of the Atlantic" and "the Stumbling Block" since at least the day the Dutch ship Palatine was wrecked near the island. The crew had mutinied, the captain had been murdered, and the passengers were starving. After they were rescued, the ship was set afire and cast adrift—but one woman was still aboard, and her screams could be heard as the burning ship floated back to sea. The sight of a ghostly ship, and the sounds of a woman screaming, still are periodically reported by mariners near here.

Left: Well before the original Block Island North Light was built in 1829, the locals would build signal fires on the shoreline—not to warn ships, but to lure them to the rocks, where their valuable cargoes could be salvaged.

British colonial government to torture and execute political prisoners. Embarrassed when such prisoners called out their defiance of the king at public hangings, the British moved the executions to a secluded rock reef off Manhasset Neck. There the prisoners were chained to iron rings to drown with the incoming tide. Legend had it that the spirits of those killed took their revenge when a shipload of British soldiers foundered on the rocks, and all aboard were drowned. Because of this legacy, keepers assigned to the lighthouse later built at Execution Rocks were allowed to request an unconditional transfer at any time.

Madness and Loneliness

Granting transfers from Execution Rocks was a rare official acknowledgment of the psychological anxiety that came with lighthouse work. But there were plenty of reminders that it was a stressful job. Mills Gunderson, keeper of Stage Harbor Light on Cape Cod, committed suicide in 1918 by hanging himself in a shed. Nils Nelson, assistant keeper at Southwest Ledge (New Haven Breakwater) Light in Connecticut, chased keeper Jorgen Jonneson around the lighthouse with a fire ax on one occasion and threatened him with a butcher's knife on another. In 1908, Nelson also took his own life.

In the mid-1800s, the keeper at Boon Island Light in Maine fell ill and died almost immediately after taking the job, leaving his young wife alone with his body on the barren offshore scrap of land. Despite fatigue and grief, she kept the lights lit, night after night, until one night the lamp went out. Fishermen who landed on the island to see what was wrong found the new widow wandering outside, insane. She died soon afterward.

At Seguin Island Light in Maine, the wife of the new keeper couldn't stand living at the isolated lighthouse. To appease her, he arranged to buy a player piano. When it arrived, however, there was only one piece of music, and she played it over and over for hours at a time. Finally driven mad, the keeper strangled his wife and took an ax to the piano. Later keepers reported hearing a phantom piano playing.

Charles L. Knight, keeper at Hendricks Head Light in Maine, told of happening across a stranger one night on the long, lonely walk to the post office. She ignored his greeting, and he went about his business, but with a feeling of dread he couldn't explain. "Never before had a night been so spooky to me as I wound my way over the long seawall by the low beaches. I had an undefined sense of uneasiness," he later said. The next day, when the tide went out, the woman's drowned body was discovered, weighted with a flatiron. "I think an affair like this is always especially gruesome to those who live way off in isolated places," Knight said. Afterward, he said, "There was a dread of passing along the lonely road at night and neighbors passing to and fro would cast anxious glances behind them." One night, Knight also heard the screams of a woman "who was no doubt in the hands of rumrunners in a motorboat passing down the river. There was no powerboat at the light that would allow us to give them a chase, so we had to sit and listen."

Maine's Wood Island Light was considered cursed since the 1896 murder of a deputy sheriff on the island by a lobsterman who then committed suicide. Near Isles of Shoals (White Island) Light in New Hampshire, a robber by the name of Louis Wagner was surprised during a robbery attempt in 1873 and killed two women whose husbands were away. Wagner escaped to the mainland but was captured, tried, and hanged.

Some keepers staved off their loneliness with pets, which occasionally became famous. In the 1930s, for example, a springer spaniel named Spot loved to ring the fog bell at Owl's Head Light in Maine whenever he heard ship's horns in the distance. One night, Spot scratched at the door to be let out, ran to the beach, and barked into the night. Three sharp blasts responded. It was the Rockland mail boat, lost in a fog, which Spot had saved from grounding on the rocks. When he died, the dog was buried near the fog bell. In the early 1900s, a dog named Smut helped save the lives of two fishermen caught in a nor'easter near Two Bush Island Light in Maine by guiding them to safety with his barking. "It sounded to us like the voice of an angel," one said. The two fishermen begged the keeper to sell them the dog at any price, but he refused.

Milo, a Newfoundland–Saint Bernard mix who lived at Egg Rock Light in Massachusetts in the 1850s, loved to retrieve objects in the water. Local fishermen tied cod to pieces of wood, which Milo would retrieve for the keeper's dinner. Milo also swam after loons the keeper shot. One day a loon fell to the ocean wounded but still able to fly for short distances. Milo chased it repeatedly until he had swum from sight. Feared lost, Milo swam back to the island the next day, after having spent the night on the mainland.

Pirates, Presidents, and Dead Ducks

Pirate yarns abound in the lore of northeastern lighthouses. Blackbeard was rumored to have hidden his treasure near what is now Maine's Hendricks Head Light. Captain Kidd was said to have left his loot near where

Thacher Island in Massachusetts, site of the twin Thacher Island (Cape Ann) Lights, was named for Anthony Thacher in 1635 as compensation after all five of his children drowned in front of his eyes in a shipwreck as they were traveling by sea from Ipswich to Marblehead.

Beavertail Light now stands in Rhode Island, on Great Captain Island in Connecticut, and on Star Island in the Isles of Shoals. In fact, a one-time owner of Star Island, Samuel Haley, found several bars of silver worth the 1930s fortune of $3,000, which he used to build a seawall, wharf, and breakwater. And Kidd was known to have friends who lived near the site of Beavertail Light, where he visited in 1696, shortly before being captured and hanged. In 1879, boys walking near Chatham Light in Massachusetts found two clay pits filled with ancient coins.

There are countless other legends of the lights. Mafia gangster Joseph Baron, also known as Joe Barboza, hid under guard near Thacher Island (Cape Ann) Lights in Massachusetts in 1967 while he was testifying against his former associates. He eventually disappeared into the witness protection program. Thacher Island keeper Maurice Babcock saved the SS *America* from crashing on the island in a fog in 1919, rushing to the foghorn as he saw the ship approaching. The ship carried a valuable cargo: President Woodrow Wilson, traveling back to Washington from the Versailles negotiations at the close of World War I.

Eight years later, the keepers at Saddleback Ledge Light in Maine were discussing World War I in the kitchen after dinner. Suddenly a barrage of blows was thundering against the tower. "We thought another war had started," keeper W. W. Wells said. Rushing outside, they found that 124 flying ducks, attracted by the light, had crashed into the tower at full speed. One, a ten-pound drake, went through the lantern glass and pierced the lens. It was, Wells said, "the weirdest experience I have had since being in the service."

Something similar happened to William W. Williams, keeper of Boon Island Light in Maine. Prevented by the weather from rowing ashore for supplies, Williams found himself without a Thanksgiving turkey as the holiday approached. Resigned to a meal of boiled potatoes and bread, he suddenly heard a flock of ducks smash providentially against the tower. Williams enjoyed a festive Thanksgiving after all.

LITERARY LIGHTS:
LIGHTHOUSES IN LITERATURE AND ART

When a new private owner drastically remodeled the white gingerbread-trimmed keeper's cottage at Cape Elizabeth Light in Maine in 1998, the *New York Times* decried the destruction of "an icon of American art." The lighthouse and its keepers cottage, after all, had been immortalized in the famous 1929 Edward Hopper painting *The Lighthouse at Two Lights*, which hangs in New York's Metropolitan Museum of Art. So distinctive was the image, it was used on a postage stamp in 1970 to commemorate the 150th anniversary of Maine's statehood.

The outcry over the sad fate of the Cape Elizabeth keeper's house was a dramatic example of how lighthouses have transcended their role as navigational aids to become singularly American symbols that have captured the imaginations of artists, writers, poets, photographers, and even filmmakers, drawn to the sense of danger, hardship, and isolation and the awe-inspiring natural coastal settings of the lights.

Ten Pound Island Light in Massachusetts was the subject of paintings by Fitzhugh Lane and Winslow Homer; Homer boarded in 1880 with the keeper at neighboring Eastern Point Light. Hopper also painted Portland Head Light, and his 1916 depiction of Maine's Monhegan Island Light was used to reconstruct the assistant keeper's cottage decades later. Among the many artists influenced by Monhegan Islands, and other islands on the Maine coast, was Andrew Winter, who lived and painted there in the 1940s. The museum now housed at Monhegan Light commemorates the island's art colony with works by such other former residents as Rockwell Kent and George Bellows.

Henry Wadsworth Longfellow took what he called his weekly walking "constitutionals" to Portland Head Light. It was at this favorite spot that he was impelled to write his poem "The Lighthouse," which reads in part:

And as the evening darkens, lo! How bright;
Through the deep purple of the twilight air,
Beams forth the sudden radiance of its light
With strange unearthly splendor in its glare!

Seguin Island Light near the mouth of the Kennebec River in Maine as painted in 1940 by Andrew Winter, who specialized in depictions of the New England coast. (Collection of the Farnsworth Art Museum. Gift of Mr. and Mrs. Leo Meissner, 1971.)

And the great ships sail outward and return
Bending and blowing o'er the billowy swells;
And ever joyful, as they see it burn,
They wave their silent welcomes and farewells.

The poet and playwright Edna St. Vincent Millay also lived in sight of Portland Head, and Sarah Orne Jewett, another neighbor, described the same coast in her book *Pearl of Orr's Island*. "You are riding in a lonely road, by some bay that seems to you like a secluded inland lake; you check your horse to notice the fine outline of the various points, when lo! from behind one of them, swan-like, with wings all spread, glides in a ship from India or China, and wakes up the silence, by tumbling her great anchor into the water," Jewett wrote.

Longfellow also visited Minot's Ledge Light, hoisted to the entrance in a sling. "The lighthouse rises out of the sea like a beautiful stone cannon, mouth upward, belching forth only friendly fires," he wrote.

Montauk Point Light on a high bluff at the lonely east-

At rather early candle-light, he lighted a small Japan lamp, allowing it to smoke rather more than we like on ordinary occasions, and told us to follow him. We ascended by a winding and open iron stairway, with a steadily increasing scent of oil and lamp-smoke, to a trap door in an iron floor, and through this into the lantern. . . .

The light consisted of fifteen Argand lamps, placed within smooth concave reflectors twenty-one inches in diameter and arranged in two horizontal circles, one above the other, facing every way except directly down the Cape.

Nathaniel Hawthorne and William Henry Dana, author of *Two Years Before the Mast*, visited the Isles of Shoals and the lighthouse on White Island. Whether by their influence or not, Celia Laighton Thaxter, daughter of the keeper, became a well-known New England writer in her own right. Not surprisingly, lighthouses were a major theme for Thaxter. She wrote a poem describing the night the *Pocahontas* went aground with no survivors in 1839, shortly after passing the Isles of Shoals:

> *Sighing I climbed the lighthouse stair,*
> *Half forgetting my grief and pain;*
> *And while the day died, sweet and fair,*
> *I lit the lamps again.*

In her book *Among the Isles of Shoals*, Thaxter remembered arriving at the lighthouse for the first time. "We were set ashore on that loneliest, lovely rock, where the lighthouse looked down on us like some tall, black-capped giant," she wrote. "Someone began to light the lamps in the tower. Red and golden, they swung around in mid-air; everything was strange and fascinating and new. . . . The cottage windows were ruddy from the glow within. I felt so much a part of the Lord's universe, I was no more afraid of the dark than the wave or the winds." The lighthouse itself she described as "a slender column against the sky. It looms colossal in the mirage of summer; in winter it lies blurred and ghostly at the edge of the chilly sea."

True stories about the lights often were transformed into poetry and fiction. John Greenleaf Whittier in 1865 wrote a narrative poem about the tragedy of the *Palatine*, which was discovered abandoned by its crew near Block Island, its passengers starving and near death. Residents who rescued the survivors lit the wreck afire and set it adrift, only to discover, horrified, that a woman remained on board.

F. Hopkinson Smith, who oversaw the supposedly impossible task of building Race Rock Light off Long Island, wrote a book about it, *Caleb Smith, Master Diver*, which was actually the story of his friend, Captain Tom Scott, who had helped to build the underwater foundation. The tale of the *Nottingham Galley*, wrecked on Maine's Boon Island, was fictionalized by Kenneth Roberts in the novel *Boon Is-*

Daughter of the keeper at Isles of Shoals (White Island) Light, Celia Laighton Thaxter became a well-known writer who made lighthouses a major theme of her work. (Courtesy of Jeremy D'Entremont)

ern point of Long Island was memorialized by Walt Whitman in his epic poem *Leaves of Grass*. "I stand as on some mighty eagle's beak," he wrote:

> *Eastward the sea absorbing, viewing nothing but sea and sky,*
> *The tossing waves, the foam, the ships in the distance,*
> *The wild unrest, the snowy, curling caps—that inbound urge and urge of waves,*
> *Seeking the shores forever.*

From the library of his house in Kittery, Maine, William Dean Howells, author of *The Rise of Silas Lapham*, could "see two lighthouses, one on each side of a foamy reef; three sails are sliding across the smooth waters within the reef, and far beyond it lie the Isles of Shoals in full sight. Could you ask more?" Among the visitors who shared the view were Henry James and Mark Twain. So inspiring is the view that Howells's house is now owned by Harvard University, which uses it as a faculty retreat.

Highland (Cape Cod) Light had Henry David Thoreau as a guest on three separate occasions. "We wished to make the most of so novel experience, and therefore told our host that we would like to accompany him when he went to light up," Thoreau recounted in his book *Cape Cod*:

land.

In the late 1930s, author Ruth Carmen wrote a book about the 1932 birth of Georgia Norwood, daughter of the keeper at Boston Light in Boston Harbor. A doctor made a trip to the island lighthouse in the middle of a storm to deliver the baby, who didn't actually come into the world until another week passed and the seas were calm. Nonetheless, Carmen called her book *Storm Child* and added other touches, most notably the destruction of the lighthouse by a tidal wave. The book was such a success that there was talk of a movie.

It was not the only time that Hollywood would be attracted to the lights. Graves Light in Boston Harbor served as the location for David O. Selznick's 1948 *Portrait of Jennie*, with Joseph Cotton, Ethel Barrymore, and Lillian Gish. Edgartown Harbor Light was featured in *Jaws*, and Brant Point Light in the 1996 film *To Gillian on Her Thirty-seventh Birthday*. And when producers needed a symbolic ending point to punctuate Tom Hanks' cross-country run in *Forrest Gump*, they, too, chose a lighthouse: Maine's Marshall Point Light.

Many legends are associated with the Thacher Island (Cape Ann) Lights. By desperately sounding the foghorn, keeper Maurice Babcock is credited with saving President Woodrow Wilson when Wilson was traveling back to Washington aboard the S.S. America *from the Versailles negotiations at the close of World War I. Mafia gangster Joseph Baron, also known as Joe Barboza, was hidden here under guard in 1967 while he was testifying against his ex-associates, before he disappeared into the witness protection program.*

The origin of the name of Rhode Island's Point Judith Light is in dispute, but a favorite tale has it that a sea captain, lost in fog at a time before there was a lighthouse at the site, shouted to his daughter to direct him toward land, purportedly shouting: "Point, Judy. Point!"

Isle Au Haut (Robinson Point) Light in Maine is on an island named by the French explorer Samuel Champlain, who was impressed by its great height. The lighthouse was renovated in 1999.

Hospital Point Light in Massachusetts is on the site of a former smallpox hospital. Today it serves as the official quarters of the commander of the First U.S. Coast Guard District and his family.

The pirate Captain Kidd was said to have left some of his treasure on Great Captain Island in Connecticut, but that's not how the island, or its lighthouse, got their names. The island was owned by Captain Daniel Patrick, who named it as a tribute — to himself.

Maine's Wood Island Light has been considered cursed since the 1896 murder of a deputy sheriff there by a lobsterman who then committed suicide.

CHAPTER 5

Rescuing the Rescuers:

Preserving the Lights

Left: *Montauk Point Light in New York now has a museum in the former keeper's quarters and the tower, which includes the radio room, oil room, and classic spiral staircase to the lantern room. There also is a model showing twenty-eight light stations from Manhattan to Point Judith, Rhode Island. With walls seven feet thick at the base and a foundation thirteen feet deep, the lighthouse is among the sturdiest in the Northeast, but dramatic steps have had to be taken to protect it from the ever increasing problem of erosion.*

Above: *Visitors are allowed into the lantern room at Gay Head Light on Martha's Vineyard, now maintained by the Martha's Vineyard Historical Society.*

No ship that ever passed beneath the emerald green beacon of Block Island Southeast Light moved this slowly: just 360 feet in two-and-a-half weeks. A glacier's pace. Slower than a snail. But onlookers held their breath as if they were watching a race. Which, in fact, they were. The 120-year-old, five-story, 2,000-ton lighthouse itself was being moved from the edge of a bluff in a race against erosion.

The endless action of the waves had washed away 250 feet of shoreline since the light was first constructed, leaving it just 55 feet from the precipice by 1984. In 1990, it had been deactivated in favor of a sterile automated beacon on a pole. As the sea continued its inexorable advance, volunteers raised $2.3 million—more than thirty times what Southeast Light had cost to build—and readied for the seemingly impossible task of dragging the enormous red brick grande dame from the brink.

First the tower's fieldstone foundation was excavated by hand. Then workers drilled holes through the bottom and inserted four gigantic I-beams knit with crossbeams. Thirty-eight sixty-ton jacks lifted the lighthouse two feet from its cobblestone foundations and lowered it onto a wheeled cradle. Seventy-five-ton rollers driven by four five-foot hydraulic jacks pushed it along a track in five-foot increments, 130 feet to the north, then 130 feet to the east, then another 100 feet to the north, where a new foundation waited.

More work remained to be done. Because it floated in a bed of mercury, the eleven-foot first-order Fresnel lens was considered dangerous to reuse, so the Coast Guard gingerly shipped another from Cape Lookout Light in North Carolina and reassembled it, one prism at a time, around a 1,000-watt bulb.

At one hour before sunset on August 27, 1994, as a band played, Southeast Light glowed again.

The monumental job of saving Block Island Southeast Light is only one example of the task confronting the relatively young American lighthouse preservation movement. As traditional historic lighthouse towers were abandoned in favor of less-costly beacons on steel poles or buoys, they became the prey not only of erosion, but also of vandalism, fire, bird and rodent infestation, rust, surf, winds, ice, snow, and storms.

They would not go quietly. Admirers of Seguin Island Light in Maine collected thousands of signatures persuading Congress to prevent its deactivation. After receiving hundreds of complaints, the Coast Guard dropped a plan to darken Maine's Baker Island Light. Local residents also objected when Penfield Reef Light in Connecticut was to be replaced with a beacon on a pole, and when their representatives in Congress intervened, the light was saved. At Annisquam Harbor Light in Massachusetts, thousands of signatures from fishermen and boaters thwarted plans to silence the fog signal.

The save-the-lighthouse movement also has resorted to such innovative methods as the first-of-its kind Maine Lights Program, under which three dozen Maine lighthouses were transferred by the federal government to cities, towns, and nonprofit organizations, including historical societies and conservation organizations. The U.S. Lighthouse Society took over Plymouth (Gurnet) Light in Massachusetts, where the Lighthouse Preservation Society runs Ten Pound Island Light. The Maine-based American Lighthouse Foundation—formerly the New England Lighthouse Foundation—has restored the keeper's house at Race Point Light on Cape Cod, and other structures, including the gravesite of heroic keeper Abbie Burgess Grant. It leases the Portsmouth Harbor Light in New Hampshire, and Long Point and Wood End lights in Massachusetts. A chapter has taken over and restored Plum Island Light in Massachusetts.

The work depends primarily on volunteers. Residents of Cape Ann, Massachusetts, formed the Thacher Island Association to refurbish Thacher Island (Cape Ann) Lights, whose north tower was reactivated in 1989, making it the nation's only operating twin light station. Retirees helped renovate Rose Island Light in Rhode Island, which had been badly vandalized; after eight years of repairs, it was relit on August 7, 1993. At Sakonnet Point Light in Rhode Island, volunteers removed pigeon droppings two feet deep and sandblasted and repainted the tower, which was relit on March 22, 1997, for the first time in forty-three years. Fort Pickering (Winter Island) Lighthouse in Massachusetts, badly damaged in a blizzard, was repaired by local residents and businesses.

All of New Bedford, Massachusetts, seemed to come together to refurbish long-abandoned Palmer Island Light, where arson had gutted the interior and damaged the lantern. Schoolchildren picked up twenty tons of litter, firefighters crafted a new wrought-iron spiral staircase, and a welder in the city's water department repaired the lantern. The tower was repainted by jail inmates in a work-release program. In Connecticut, the chamber of commerce raised money to restore Great Captain Island Light. And employees of major local corporations contributed their time to renovate Sheffield Island (Norwalk) Light.

Even then, there have been discouraging setbacks. Shortly after it was fixed up, Palmer Island Light was vandalized again. Almost as soon as the volunteers had left, Sheffield Island Light was badly damaged by a storm that smashed windows, flooded the basement, and tossed a brand-new power generator into the ocean. Black Rock Harbor (Fayerweather Island) Light in Connecticut suffered from neglect and vandalism even after local residents had pooled their time to replace the doors and windows and to landscape the site. Undaunted, they returned, repaired the masonry, installed new glass, and applied graffiti-resistant paint.

One of the earliest attempts at preservation was the least successful. After Egg Rock Light in Massachusetts was deactivated, it was offered for five dollars to anyone who could remove it from its island. In October 1922, as workers tried to move the building to a barge, a rope snapped, and the lighthouse sank.

Like Egg Rock, many Northeast lighthouses came to be considered surplus thanks to changes in shipping traffic and technology. Sandy Neck Light on Cape Cod, for example, was deactivated in 1931 when the shoreline shifted and nearby Barnstable Harbor declined in importance. Palmer Island Light was decommissioned when a new hurricane wall altered the configuration of New Bedford Harbor in 1963.

Nor were all lighthouses saved. A preservation group abandoned plans to renovate Cedar Island Light in New York when the county declined to build an access road. Rhode Island's Plum Beach Light, which became obsolete with the construction of the Jamestown Bridge on Narragansett Bay, was left to languish for decades because of successive legal controversies. First a worker hired to paint the tower sued after purportedly suffering eye damage. Then the state refused to take it back from the federal government. When a Massachusetts group proposed buying the lighthouse and moving it away, a local organization was finally formed to save it.

Some lights, or the land they sit on, passed to private owners. Ida Lewis Rock (Lime Rock) Light in Rhode Island, for example, is now the Ida Lewis Yacht Club. Nearby Newport Harbor (Goat Island) Light, which is automated but still active, is on the grounds of a hotel. Stage Harbor Light on Cape Cod was sold in 1933, when it was replaced by an automated beacon on a pole. Ditto Wing's Neck Light in Massachusetts and Stamford Har-

Cape Ann, Massachusetts, residents have formed an association to refurbish Thacher Island (Cape Ann) Lights, including its 1816 keeper's house, shown here with the South Tower in the background

The Thacher Island (Cape Ann) Lights were restored in 1988, and the North Tower, deactivated in 1932, was reactivated as a private aid to navigation after the restoration, making the Thacher Island (Cape Ann) Lights America's only operating twin light station. Its two stone towers stand 300 yards apart. This view shows the South Tower as seen from the North Tower, whose original first-order Fresnel lens is in the U.S. Coast Guard Academy museum in New London, Connecticut

bor (Chatham Rocks) Light in Connecticut. The island under Winter Harbor Light in Maine is privately owned. Morgan Point Light in Connecticut is now used as a private summer cottage. So is the famous keeper's house at Cape Elizabeth Light in Maine, whose new owner drastically remodeled it. Most people who buy lighthouses, however, have respected their designs. Morgan Point's new owner even ordered up a replica of the original lantern room based on U.S. Lighthouse Service blueprints. The owners of the former Bristol Ferry Light in Rhode Island not only had the lantern room rebuilt to the original specifications but also installed a beacon.

The Coast Guard has preserved some lights on its own. It restored Nantucket's Brant Point Light, for instance, and the extraordinary art-deco Cleveland East Ledge Light in Massachusetts' Buzzards Bay. Although the lamp itself is automated, Point Judith Light remains a Coast Guard station. Hospital Point Light in Massachusetts now serves as home to the commander of the First U.S. Coast Guard District, and Nobska Point Light on Cape Cod houses the commander of the Coast Guard base at Woods Hole. Chatham Light on Cape Cod, Lynde Point (Saybrook) Light in Connecticut, and others also serve as Coast Guard housing.

Some Coast Guard units also have adopted lights, voluntarily maintaining them or giving tours. The Coast Guard Auxiliary Flotilla 11-2 adopted Nobska Light, and Ned's Point Light in Massachusetts was adopted by the Coast Guard Flotilla 63, First District Northern Region.

Many coastal towns, whose histories are so bound up with nearby lights, have bought or leased them. Rockland Harbor Breakwater Light in Maine has now been transferred to the city of Rockland, whose emblem and letterhead depict the lighthouse. The town of Scituate, Massachusetts, bought the abandoned Scituate Light, reactivating it in August 1994 for the first time in 134 years. The Massachusetts town of Marion provided the money for a solar-powered flashing light to reactivate Bird Island Light on July 4, 1997. York, Maine, owns Cape Neddick ("the Nubble") Light. New Haven, Connecticut, and Mattapoisett, Massachusetts, have created public parks around Five Mile Point and Ned's Point Lights, respectively.

Two towns have chosen unique methods of preserving local lighthouses. Castine, Maine, which owns Dice Head Light, rents it to a residential tenant. Old Field, New York, uses one of the two former keeper's houses at Old Field Point Light as its village hall, and the other as

Palmer Island Light in New Bedford, Massachusetts, was deactivated when a new hurricane wall altered the configuration of the city's harbor in 1962. Victimized by vandalism, arson, and neglect, it was restored by a broad community effort involving everyone from schoolchildren to firefighters to jail inmates, who repainted the exterior. The lighthouse was rededicated on August 30, 1999, exactly 150 years to the minute after it was first lit.

One year after it was discontinued in 1927, Ida Lewis Rock Light became the headquarters of the Ida Lewis Yacht Club, which continues to shine its beacon every night between Memorial Day to Columbus Day. The original sixth-order Fresnel lens tended by heroic keeper Ida Lewis is in the Museum of Newport History.

a constable's residence.

Other lights have been converted to museums, parks, and refuges. The fog signal building at Race Point Light on Cape Cod is now a laboratory for marine research. Monhegan Island Light in Maine is part of an art museum. Maine's Grindle Point Light, a square Pacific-style lighthouse built on the Atlantic as a prototype—and re-activated after lobbying by the town of Islesboro—is home to the Sailors Memorial Museum, which exhibits some of its original whale oil lamps. The keeper's house at Pemaquid Point Light is a fishing museum, which has the original fourth-order Fresnel lens from Baker Island Light in Maine.

One of the first lighthouses to be converted into a museum was Stonington Harbor Light in Connecticut, operated by the Stonington Historical Society since 1925. The museum has rare whale oil, harpoons, and unexploded incendiary devices fired at the town by five British warships on August 9, 1814, during the darkest

days of the War of 1812. From the octagonal tower of the distinctive granite lighthouse, which is no longer used, are views of New York, Rhode Island, and Connecticut. Also in Connecticut, Sheffield Island (Norwalk) Light has been restored and furnished as it would have been when the keeper lived there with his family in 1902. New York's Montauk Point Light has a museum in the former keeper's quarters, which includes the radio room, oil room, and classic spiral staircase to the lantern room. Horton Point Light houses the Southold, New York, Historical Society Nautical Museum, with sea chests, scrimshaw, ship artifacts, and lighthouse artifacts. North of the tower rests the recovered anchor of the side-wheeler *Commodore*, which was wrecked on Christmas Day in 1866. There is a fourth-order Fresnel lens on exhibit in the keeper's quarters of New York's Fire Island Light, which also has some pieces of the original exterior of the tower. Beavertail Light in Rhode Island, has a museum in the assistant lighthouse keeper's cottage with a fourth-order Fresnel lens. Here also are models of every other lighthouse in the state. Ned's Point, Scituate, Nauset, and the nearby inactive Three Sisters lights in Massachusetts also are open to the public, and the oil house at Watch Hill Light in Rhode Island contains a small museum.

Portland Head Light, Maine's oldest lighthouse, has a museum that includes the original second-order Fresnel lens and two fourth-order lenses. The Martha's Vineyard Historical Society takes responsibility for maintaining East Chop (Telegraph Hill), West Chop, Edgartown Harbor, and Gay Head lights. At Gay Head Light, visitors are allowed into the light chamber, where they can watch the two lights rotate. East Chop Light is open to the public by appointment.

The oldest lighthouse on Cape Cod, Highland (Cape Cod) Light in Truro, allows visitors all the way up to the lantern room, sixty-nine winding steps and 183 feet above the sea. The keeper's watch room is also open to the public. On display inside the keeper's house are artifacts relating to the light, including lanterns, intact early lenses, and pieces of the original 1857 first-order Fresnel lens used here, which was largely destroyed while it was being removed. The Highland Museum 500 yards away in the former Highland House summer hotel, has a shipwreck room, historic photos of the lighthouse, general information, and more pieces of the lens.

Some of the lighthouses now are part of parks and nature areas. Wood Island, the site of Wood Island Light, is a bird sanctuary maintained by the Audubon Society. The U.S. Fish and Wildlife Service oversees the area around Monomoy Point Light on Cape Cod and Maine's Two Bush Island and Petit Manan lights. Monomoy's lighthouse is used by the Cape Cod Museum of Natural History as a nature center, and the land around it is home to more than 300 species of birds. The 3,355-acre Petit Manan National Wildlife Refuge is famous for its colony of puffins and for other birds, including Arctic terns.

Burnt Island Light in Maine has been turned over to the state for use as a maritime history, science, and navigation educational facility. Maine's West Quoddy Head Light is used as housing for the manager of Quoddy Head State Park. The Three Sisters towers that were sold and moved away from Nauset on Cape Cod in 1911 and 1923 have been repurchased by the government and restored, and they now stand idiosyncratically in a clearing surrounded by woods at the Cape Cod National Seashore. Derby Wharf Light in Massachusetts has been taken over by the Salem National Historical Park and

reactivated as a private aid to navigation.

Other lights have been preserved as overnight accommodations, with the proceeds put back into maintenance. The Cape Cod Museum of Natural History arranges stays at Monomoy Point and Race Point lights; there's no electricity or running water in either case, but a guide prepares dinner by lantern light. More luxurious accommodations are at Bass River Light on Cape Cod, now the Lighthouse Inn, with rooms in the former keeper's quarters; and at Isle Au Haut (Robinson Point) Light in Maine, now a bed-and-breakfast inn.

Some of the lights were rescued just in time. Fire Island Light, deactivated in 1974, was declared in 1981 to be unsafe and beyond repair. Three previous attempts to save it had failed. With the lighthouse scheduled for demolition, the Fire Island Lighthouse Preservation Society raised $1.2 million in four years, and on May 25, 1986, the beacon was relit. "It has become evident that the society's effort is not directed to saving the lighthouse just to save it. It is directed to saving the lighthouse to put it to work, educating us with the lessons it holds, inspiring us with the heroics of its history, and linking us with a past that can fortify us for the future," the organization's president, Thomas F. Roberts III, told the assembled crowd.

Block Island North Light was decommissioned in 1970 and sat abandoned until 1989, when it was sold to the town of New Shoreham for one dollar. Hundreds of thousands of dollars were spent removing the effects of vandalism and neglect. On August 5, 1989, the light was turned back on. The first floor was opened as a museum, which includes the original fourth-order Fresnel lens. Beavertail Light in Rhode Island also suffered from vandalism, including a gunshot that shattered its lens in 1975. It was later refurbished. When Bakers Island Light in Massachusetts was finally repaired in 1996, the contractor said that the foundation and the tower were so badly deteriorated, they would not have stood another year.

Duxbury Pier ("Bug") Light in Massachusetts also was saved at the eleventh hour. Vandals and seabirds took over the leaky structure after it was automated in 1964. By 1983, the Coast Guard had decided to remove it. Local residents, however, raised money for repairs, and the lighthouse got a major overhaul in 1996. Neighbors also protested when the Coast Guard altered the appearance of the lights by lopping off the distinctive lantern rooms to free up space for modern airport-style

beacons. In response, the Coast Guard eventually returned the lantern rooms—or at least aluminum replicas of them.

The biggest enemy of northeastern lights has proved to be erosion. The Army Corps of Engineers calculated in 1990 that Sankaty Head Light would pitch over its eroding bluff within ten years. The keeper's house and other buildings have been moved, and pipes and pumps beneath the sand have so far slowed erosion underneath the tower. Faulkners Island Light in Connecticut stood only thirty-five feet from the eroding shore when local residents persuaded the Army Corps of Engineers to build a massive stone revetment shielding as much as half of the circumference of the island. The sea had crept to within just fifty feet of Montauk Point Light by the late 1960s when trenches were dug and filled with reeds and grass to hold the bank in place.

The most drastic preservation tactic is to move the lighthouse. Colchester Reef Light, which in 1933 was deactivated and sat abandoned on its reef in Lake Champlain, was moved to the landlocked Shelburne Museum in 1952. Every piece was labeled and the light was disassembled, moved, and reassembled over several years. In 1996, the ninety-ton Nauset Light on Cape Cod was moved 300 feet from the eroding shore in response to a public outcry when the Coast Guard hinted it might be deactivated. By then, the ocean was within just 43 feet of the tower. The light was back on by May 10, 1997. The keeper's house was also moved the next year. Massachusetts' Plymouth (Gurnet) Light, the nation's oldest wooden lighthouse, was moved 140 feet from an eroding cliff in 1998. And the five-ton Doubling Point Light in Maine was lifted off of its foundation with a crane, placed on a barge, and taken to a warehouse for repairs before it was returned to its original site in 2000.

When Cape Cod's Highland (Cape Cod) Light was built in 1797, it stood 500 feet from the shore. But by the time Henry David Thoreau dropped in fifty years later, he couldn't help but notice that "this vast clay bank is fast wearing away; small streams of water trickling down it at intervals of two or three rods have left the interme-

Lynde Point (Saybrook) Light shines its beacon across the Connecticut River near Old Saybrook Harbor. Like many other lights, it now is used for housing by the U.S. Coast Guard.

Slated for demolition in 1973, Rockland Harbor Breakwater Light in Maine was rescued by a public outcry and taken over by the city of Rockland, which maintains it to this day.

diate clay in the form of steep Gothic roofs fifty feet high or more, the ridges as sharp and rugged-looking as rocks; and in one place the bank is curiously eaten out in the form of a large semicircular crater." By 1996, the cliffs had come within 100 feet and were encroaching on the light at the rate of at least three feet a year. More than $1.5 million was spent to drag the 430-ton lighthouse farther inland. The foundation was dug out, and crossbeams placed beneath the structure, which was lifted with hydraulic jacks and set on rollers greased with Ivory soap. It took eighteen days to move the lighthouse 450 feet. It was relit on November 3, 1996.

Lighthouses also have been used as symbols to preserve the shores around them. A license plate issued in 1992 by the state of Connecticut to raise money for Long Island Sound pictures Saybrook Breakwater Light. Issued to 100,000 motorists, the plate raised more than $3 million. In Massachusetts, revenues from sales of a license plate depicting Nauset Light pay for conservation planning on Cape Cod.

The enthusiasm for these lights was most apparent when they were reactivated. Thousands were on hand, including three crews of the local rowing club in whaleboats, when Palmer Island Light was rededicated on August 30, 1999, exactly 150 years to the minute after it was first lit. The largest flotilla of boats ever assembled on Long Island was on hand for the relighting of Fire Island Light. Fireworks burst over Gloucester Harbor on the night of August 7, 1989, when Ten Pound Island Light was turned back on. And when nearby Eastern Point Light was automated in September 1985, one person was given the honor of being the last person to manually activate the light. He was the grandson of the first keeper.

Deactivated in 1877, when the light at nearby Southwest Ledge went into operation, Connecticut's Five Mile Point Light was restored in 1986 and now stands at the center of New Haven's Lighthouse Point Park.

New methods are being used to control erosion at places such as Gay Head Light on Martha's Vineyard, where the underlying cliffs are slowly being stabilized. The encroaching Atlantic Ocean can be clearly seen from the lantern room.

The keeper's house of the original 1823 Old Field Point Light in Old Field, New York, is now the village hall, while the second floor of the 1868 lighthouse building that succeeded it today serves as the residence of the village constable.

A square Pacific-style lighthouse built on the Atlantic as a prototype, Grindle Point Light in Maine was decommissioned in 1934 but reactivated after lobbying by the town of Islesboro. It is now home to the Sailor's Memorial Museum, which exhibits some of the original whale oil lamps, and is furnished as it would have been when a keeper lived here.

SEEING THE LIGHTS

any of the Northeast's most interesting lighthouse artifacts aren't in lighthouses at all, but in museums, town halls, military academies, and other places you might least expect to find them. The nation's largest collection of lighthouse-related objects is in the Shore Village Museum in Rockland, Maine, including foghorns, search and rescue gear, buoys, and boats. There are also lighthouse lenses dating as far back as 1790, among them the Fresnel lenses from Petit Manan, Doubling Point, Great Point, Burnt Island, the Cuckolds, Marshall Point, Matinicus Rock, and Whitehead Island lights, and a rare sixth-order lens made by Henri LaPaute of Paris, which stands only eighteen inches high and was likely used in a river

or small harbor light. Housed in a former Coast Guard barracks, the museum also has the bell from the original Nantucket lightship, sunk in 1934 in a collision with the *Titanic's* sister ship, *Olympic*.

The U.S. Coast Guard Academy in New London, Connecticut, has a little-known museum that boasts one of the only first-order Fresnel lenses on display in the United States, originally installed in one of the Thacher Island lighthouse towers near Cape Ann, Massachusetts. There are also artifacts from the history of the Coast Guard and its predecessors—the Life Saving Service, the Steamboat Inspection Service, the Lighthouse Establishment, and the Revenue Cutter Service—including cannons, uniforms, links from the chain that colonists stretched across the Hudson River at West Point to keep the British navy from moving upriver, models of Coast Guard icebreakers, World War II propaganda posters, and movie posters from unlikely Hollywood adventure films about the Coast Guard, such as *Don Winslow of the Coast Guard*, and *Sea Spoilers*, with John Wayne. Also on display is America's biggest and grandest tall ship, *Eagle*, originally commissioned in Hamburg in 1936 to train German navy cadets before World War II, when it was converted to a cargo ship and ultimately seized by the United States. *Eagle* is open for tours when it is in port, generally from late summer through early spring; its gigantic figurehead hangs in the museum.

Another first-order Fresnel lens has been retired to a specially built miniature lighthouse tower on the grounds of the Martha's Vineyard Historical Society museum. This lens, with 1,009 individual prisms to maximize the beam's intensity, was originally installed in the Gay Head Lighthouse in 1856 after first being exhibited at the World's Fair

These Fresnel lenses are on display at the Shore Village Museum in Rockland, Maine, which has the largest collection of lighthouse artifacts in the United States, including foghorns, rescue gear, buoys, boats, and lenses dating back to 1790. Housed in a former Coast Guard barracks, it also features Coast Guard artifacts and the bell from the original Nantucket lightship, sunk in 1934 in a collision with the Titanic's sister ship, Olympic.

in Paris. The society's museum complex also includes the twelve-room Thomas Cooke House, which has logbooks, ship models, scrimshaw, harpoons, and treasures brought back from the South Pacific, including carved ceremonial artifacts. Outside, in the carriage shed, is a whaleboat once used for racing in the harbor, and a Hawaiian outrigger canoe brought back by whalers as a souvenir.

The original 1856 sixth-order Fresnel lens from Brant Point Light and the 1857 third-order lens from Great Point Light are on display in the Nantucket Life Saving Museum, which also has such distinctive artifacts as drip pans used to catch the oil from beneath the light, a 1930s keeper's cap, and U.S. Lighthouse Service china. It also has one of the last four surviving Massachusetts Humane Society surf boats, the only horsedrawn beach rescue cart, quarterboards from wrecked ships, and relics from one of the greatest wrecks of all, that of the luxurious Italian passenger liner *Andrea Doria*, which sank after being struck by the Swedish-American liner *Stockholm* in a thick Nantucket fog on July 25, 1956. The second-order lens from the Sankaty Head Light is in the nearby Nantucket Whaling Museum, which also displays baskets woven by the bored crewmen of the nineteenth-century Nantucket lightships.

A nineteenth-century keeper's cap and uniform brass buttons, buoy lanterns, and lighthouse models built by author and historian Edward Rowe Snow are in the Hull, Massachusetts, Lifesaving Museum, along with the 1871 fourth-order Fresnel lens from Plymouth (Gurnet) Light in Plymouth Bay, the nation's oldest wooden lighthouse. The *Nantasket*, another of the four surviving surfboats built for the Massachusetts Humane Society, is also in the museum, which itself is housed in the former Point Allerton U.S. Lifesaving Station, directly facing Boston Light. The story goes that Joshua James, considered the greatest American lifesaver with 1,000 rescues to his credit, died of a heart attack while stepping out of this boat on March 19, 1902, when he was seventy-five. The museum has other historic rescue equipment, a radio room, and rescue medals.

The beacon from the Lime Rock Light, whose most famous keeper was Ida Lewis, is in the Museum of Newport History in Newport, Rhode Island. The Long Island Maritime Museum in West Sayville, New York, includes artifacts from the lifesaving service and maps of all Long Island shipwrecks. Mystic Seaport in Connecticut has a full-scale copy of the lighthouse at Brant Point in Nantucket. The copy, like the original, is equipped with a fourth-order Fresnel lens. Lake Champlain's Colchester Reef Light is at the Shelburne Museum in Shelburne, Vermont, where it was moved in 1952.

Housed in the former cannon repair shop of nineteenth-century Fort Preble, which stood on this site, the Portland Harbor Museum in Maine has its own entire lighthouse, the 1897 Spring Point Ledge Light, the only caisson-style lighthouse in the United States accessible by foot—in this case, across a breakwater. Occasional tours of the keeper's quarters and watch rooms are offered in the summer as fundraising events for the museum, which also has a nine-foot acetylene-powered buoy lens and other lighthouse lenses.

Some lighthouse artifacts turn up in the least-expected places. The spectacular second-order Fresnel lens from Cape Elizabeth Light in Maine is in the Cape Elizabeth Town Hall, for example.

There's even a museum that was inspired by a painting of a lighthouse: the Monhegan Museum in Monhegan, Maine, which took its vision from a 1916 Edward Hopper painting of the island's lighthouse with its assistant keeper's cottage, since demolished. That led to the idea of reconstructing the cottage just as Hopper painted it to house an art collection and historical mementos, including the American flag that covered the coffin of the Monhegan Island Lighthouse keeper's son, who died fighting in the Civil War.

———————————◦———————————

Shore Village Museum, 104 Limerock Street, Rockland, Maine
Open daily 10 A.M. to 4 P.M., June 1 through October 15;
October 16 through May 31 by appointment; 207-594-0311

Coast Guard Museum, U.S. Coast Guard Academy, Mohegan
Avenue, New London, Connecticut
Open Monday through Friday 9 A.M. to 5 P.M., Saturday 10 A.M.
to 5 P.M., Sunday noon to 5 P.M.; 860-444-8511

Martha's Vineyard Historical Society, 59 School Street,
Edgartown, Massachusetts
Open Tuesday through Saturday 10 A.M. to 5 P.M., June 5
through Columbus Day; then Wednesday through Friday 1 P.M.
to 4 P.M. and Saturday 10 A.M. to 4 P.M.; 508-627-4441

Nantucket Lifesaving Museum, 159 Polpis Road, Nantucket,
Massachusetts
Open daily 9:30 A.M. to 4 P.M., mid-June through Columbus
Day; 508-228-1885

Nantucket Whaling Museum, 5 Broad Street, Nantucket,
Massachusetts
Open daily 10 A.M. to 5 P.M., May 1 through Columbus Day;
508-228-1736

Hull Lifesaving Museum, 1117 Nantasket Avenue, Hull,
Massachusetts
Open Wednesday through Sunday 10 A.M. to 5 P.M., Memorial
Day through Labor Day; then Friday through Sunday 10 A.M. to
4 P.M.; 781-925-5433

Museum of Newport History, Washington Square, 127 Thames
Street, Newport, Rhode Island

Open Monday and Wednesday through Saturday 10 A.M. to 5
P.M., Sunday 1 P.M. to 5 P.M., May 1 through October 31; call for
hours November 1 through April 30; 401-846-0813

Long Island Maritime Museum, 86 West Avenue, West Sayville,
New York
Open Wednesday through Saturday 10 A.M. to 3 P.M., Sunday
noon to 4 P.M.; 631-854-4974

Mystic Seaport, 75 Greenmanville Avenue, Mystic, Connecticut
Ships and exhibits open daily 10 A.M. to 4 P.M., museum grounds
open daily 9 A.M. to 5 P.M.; 888-973-2767

Shelburne Museum, Route 7, Shelburne, Vermont
Open daily 1 P.M. to 4 P.M., April 1 through mid-May; daily 10
A.M. to 5 P.M., mid-May through mid-October; daily 1 P.M. to 4
P.M., mid-October through mid-December; 802-985-3346

Portland Harbor Museum, Southern Maine Technical College,
Fort Road, South Portland, Maine
Open daily 10 A.M. to 4:30 P.M., July and August; call for hours
in May, June, and September through December; 207-799-6337

Cape Elizabeth Town Hall, 320 Ocean House Road, Cape
Elizabeth, Maine
Open 7:30 A.M. to 5 P.M. Monday, 7:30 A.M. to 4 P.M. Tuesday
through Friday; 207-799-5251

Monhegan Museum, Lighthouse Hill, Monhegan Island, Maine
Open 11:30 A.M. to 3 P.M., July 1 through October 1; 207-596-
7003

Above: *A New England landmark that stands near the east-ernmost point of the continental United States, West Quoddy Head Light in Maine is now maintained by the Maine Division of Natural Resources; the manager of Quoddy Head State Park lives in the keeper's house.*

Right: *Threatened by the encroachment of erosion, the keeper's house and other buildings at Sankaty Head Light on Nantucket have been moved, and the U.S. Army Corps of Engineers calculated in 1990 that the Sankaty Head Light tower would pitch over its eroding bluff within ten years. But pipes and pumps beneath the sand have managed to stabilize the Sankaty bluffs.*

Above: Colchester Reef Light on Lake Champlain in Vermont was deactivated and abandoned in 1933, and fell into disrepair. Nearly twenty years later, it was disassembled, moved, and reassembled at the landlocked Shelburne Museum in Shelburne, Vermont. (Courtesy of Jeremy D'Entremont. Reprinted by permission of Dorothy Bicknell.)

Right: Every piece of the Colchester Reef Light was carefully labeled, but it took years to reassemble the lighthouse in its new home, the Shelburne Museum, beginning in 1952. Today, exhibits inside re-create what it was like to live in a lake lighthouse.

Marking the entrance to the York River, the forty-one-foot, cast-iron Cape Neddick ("the Nubble") Light was built in 1879 on a tiny rocky island called "the Nubble." Automated in 1987, it was taken over by the town of York in 1997.

Guide to New England and Long Island Lighthouses

Maine

Baker Island Light

NEAR ISLESFORD

ESTABLISHED: 1828

A wooden lighthouse was built on Baker Island in 1828 to warn of dangerous ledges and shallow sandbars on the approach to Frenchman Bay. Replaced in 1855 by the existing forty-three-foot brick tower, the light was automated in 1966. The grounds are open to the public in the summer.

Bass Harbor Head Light

MOUNT DESERT ISLAND

ESTABLISHED: 1858

Perched on a ledge on the southwest point of Mount Desert Island, Bass Harbor Head Light guides vessels into Blue Hill Bay and Bass Harbor. The thirty-two-foot lighthouse tower and accompanying keeper's house were built in 1858. The light was automated in 1974, but still has the fourth-order Fresnel lens that was installed in 1902. The grounds are adjacent to Acadia National Park and are open to the public.

Bear Island (Northeast Harbor) Light

NEAR NORTHEAST HARBOR

ESTABLISHED: 1839

DEACTIVATED: 1981

This modest thirty-one-foot white-brick lighthouse, built in 1889, was the third to be located here. The present tower and its original keeper's quarters overlook a breath-taking piece of coastline, now part of Acadia National Park. Replaced by a buoy in 1981, it was renovated and reactivated by a private group in time for its centennial in 1989.

Curtis Island Light in Maine

Blue Hill Bay Light

NEAR BROOKLIN

ESTABLISHED: 1857

DEACTIVATED: 1933

Overlooking the home town of *Charlotte's Web* author E. B. White, the original white brick Blue Hill Bay Light with its keeper's quarters now serve together as a private summer house, having been deactivated in 1933 and replaced by a light on a high pole two years later.

Boon Island Light

NEAR YORK

ESTABLISHED: 1799

This desolate, uninhabited rock surrounded by danger-ous ledges has been the site of a lighthouse since 1799, when a fifty-foot wooden tower was constructed. Twice demolished by storms, the present lighthouse dates from 1855 and is the tallest in New England, at 133 feet. Pow-erful weather continues to affect the island to this day. The light was automated two years after the blizzard of 1978 caused extensive damage; the boathouse was de-stroyed in a 1991 storm.

Browns Head Light

VINALHAVEN

ESTABLISHED: 1832

Only twenty feet tall, this white brick lighthouse is shorter than its adjacent keeper's quarters, but is perched high on the northwest end of Vinalhaven Island, whose quar-ries produced the granite for such landmarks as the Wash-ington Monument, the base of the Brooklyn Bridge, and the Cathedral of St. John the Divine in New York. Built in 1857, it is still in use, complete with a 1902 fourth-order Fresnel lens, though it was automated in 1987. The original fog bell is in the Vinalhaven Historical Society museum.

Burnt Coat Harbor (Hockamock Head) Light
SWANS ISLAND
ESTABLISHED: 1872
Originally one of a pair of range lights, the square brick Burnt Coat Harbor Light remains in operation, though its twin was torn down in 1884. Automated in 1975, the tower is now owned by the town.

Burnt Island Light
BOOTHBAY
ESTABLISHED: 1821
Burnt Island Light has stood at the west side of the entrance to Boothbay Harbor since 1821. In 1962, it became the last lighthouse in New England to be converted to electricity, and in 1989, it was one of the last to be automated. The grounds are open to the public.

Cape Elizabeth Light
CAPE ELIZABETH
ESTABLISHED: 1828
WEST TOWER DEACTIVATED: 1924
Built in 1828, the two sixty-five-foot stone towers at Cape Elizabeth comprised the first twin lights in Maine. In 1874, the two towers were replaced with new, slightly taller cast-iron models. The west light was switched off permanently in 1924 and was later sold to private owners. The east light was automated in 1963 and is inside Two Lights State Park. The keeper's house also was sold and has been drastically remodeled.

Cape Neddick ("the Nubble") Light
YORK
ESTABLISHED: 1879
Marking the entrance to the York River, the forty-one-foot cast-iron Cape Neddick Light was built in 1879 on a tiny rocky island fishermen nicknamed the Nubble. Automated in 1987, it still has a fourth-order Fresnel lens dating from 1891. The lighthouse was taken over by the town of York in 1997.

Cuckolds Light
SOUTHPORT
ESTABLISHED: 1892
Named after a point on the Thames River in England that was owned by a man whose wife purportedly had an affair with the king, the Cuckolds are a pair of ledges near the approach to Boothbay Harbor. There was originally only a small circular fog signal building on this barren spit of coast; when a lighthouse was needed in 1907, a lantern was simply built on top of it. The original fourth-order Fresnel lens is now at the Shore Village Museum in Rockland, Maine.

Curtis Island Light
CAMDEN
ESTABLISHED: 1835
Named for Cyrus Curtis, publisher of the *Saturday Evening Post*, Curtis Island sits off the Camden Harbor entrance from Penobscot Bay—making it a perfect location for a lighthouse. The current lighthouse, built in 1896, was automated in 1972. The original fourth-order Fresnel lens is on display in the Camden Public Library.

Deer Island Thorofare (Mark Island) Light
STONINGTON
ESTABLISHED: 1857
A twenty-five-foot square brick tower, this lighthouse was automated in 1958 and is now surrounded by a bird sanctuary.

Dice Head Light
CASTINE
ESTABLISHED: 1829
DEACTIVATED: 1937
Dice Head Light was built in 1829 to mark the mouth of the Penobscot River. With the decline of shipping traffic on the river, it was decommissioned in 1937 and replaced by a twenty-seven-foot steel tower at the harbor entrance. The lighthouse and keeper's quarters are now owned by the town and are open for group tours by appointment; call 207-326-4502.

Doubling Point Light
ARROWSIC
ESTABLISHED: 1899
Along with the range lights on this island, Doubling Point Light helps guide Kennebec River traffic. Damaged by ice floes, it was removed intact in 1999, repaired, and returned to its newly restored granite foundation. The light was automated in 1988; its original fourth-order Fresnel lens is at the Shore Village Museum in Rockland, Maine.

Doubling Point Range Lights
ARROWSIC
ESTABLISHED: 1898
Known collectively as the Kennebec River Light Station, these two tiny wooden towers (both are only thir-

Dusk at Chatham Light on Cape Cod

teen feet tall) sit on marshy Arrowsic Island, warning vessels on the Kennebec River to keep clear. Two of a series of lighthouses built along the Kennebec in 1898, they were automated in 1980.

Eagle Island Light
NEAR DEER ISLAND
ESTABLISHED: 1838
This thirty-foot lighthouse overlooks eastern Penobscot Bay from a high cliff. The keeper's house was torn down in 1959, and the tower was automated in 1963.

Egg Rock Light
WINTER HARBOR
ESTABLISHED: 1875
A forty-foot brick tower rising from the center of a wooden keeper's house, Egg Rock Light was built in 1875 at the entrance to Frenchman Bay. Despite suffering through

monumental storms, it remained more or less unaltered until the Coast Guard removed the lantern to make room for an airport-style beacon in 1976. After a public outcry, Egg Rock Light was restored to its original appearance ten years later. It is inside Acadia National Park.

Fort Point Light
STOCKTON SPRINGS
ESTABLISHED: 1837
On the west side of the mouth of the Penobscot River, Fort Point Light was named for an adjacent colonial-era fort. Originally a granite tower, it was replaced by the existing thirty-one-foot square brick lighthouse in 1857. Although Fort Point Light was automated in 1988, the fourth-order Fresnel lens installed in 1837 remains in place; now inside Fort Point Park, the grounds are open to the public, though the lighthouse itself is not.

Fort Point Light in Maine reflected in a window of the bell tower

Franklin Island Light

NEAR FRIENDSHIP

ESTABLISHED: 1805

The third lighthouse site in Maine, Franklin Island Light directs mariners in Muscongus Bay. The existing forty-five-foot brick tower was built in 1855 and automated in 1967. Its original fourth-order Fresnel lens is now on display at the Coast Guard station in Boothbay Harbor.

Goat Island Light

CAPE PORPOISE

ESTABLISHED: 1835

Goat Island Light is in Cape Porpoise Harbor, named for the schools of porpoises that once were common there. The existing twenty-five-foot white brick tower, which dates from 1859, marks dangerous rocks there. It was the last manned lighthouse in the country except for Boston Light when it was finally automated in 1990.

During the presidency of George Bush, the lighthouse served as an outpost for Secret Service agents guarding his estate at Walker's Point.

Goose Rocks Light

NEAR NORTH HAVEN

ESTABLISHED: 1890

One of four cast-iron "spark plug" lighthouses in Maine—three of which survive—the fifty-one-foot Goose Rocks Light stands alongside a busy sea route between Vinalhaven and North Haven. It was automated in 1963.

Great Duck Island Light

NEAR MOUNT DESERT ISLAND

ESTABLISHED: 1890

Named for the huge flock of ducks that came there every spring to raise their young, isolated Great Duck Island helps guide ships through the approach to Blue Hill Bay. The lantern at the top of the forty-two-foot cylindrical granite tower was automated in 1986, and the lighthouse is now solar powered. The keeper's house is maintained by the College of the Atlantic, which conducts ecological research there.

Grindle Point Light

ISLESBORO

ESTABLISHED: 1850

DEACTIVATED: 1934 (REACTIVATED IN 1987)

Built in 1850 to mark the entrance to Islesboro's Gilkey Harbor, Grindle Point Light was replaced in 1874 with the existing thirty-nine-foot square brick tower attached to a wooden keeper's house. Decommissioned in 1934 in favor of a beacon on a metal tower, the lighthouse was reactivated in 1987. The building now houses the Sailor's Memorial Museum, which is furnished as it would have been when the keeper lived there; call 207-734-2253 for more information.

Halfway Rock Light

NEAR SOUTH HARPSWELL

ESTABLISHED: 1871

Halfway Rock, a ledge in the middle of Casco Bay, presented an engineering challenge to the builders of its lighthouse, who ultimately followed the model of Minot's Ledge Light in Massachusetts by constructing a seventy-six-foot tower with granite blocks dovetailed together. The lighthouse was automated in 1975; in 1991, a storm washed away every other structure on the ledge.

Visitors watch the sunset from the lantern tower of Gay Head Light on Martha's Vineyard

Hendricks Head Light
WEST SOUTHPORT
ESTABLISHED: 1829
DEACTIVATED: 1935 (REACTIVATED IN 1951)
Originally a tower on top of a granite keeper's house, Hendricks Head Light was replaced in 1875 with the existing thirty-nine-foot square brick tower. Deactivated in 1933, the lighthouse was sold, but when the owners added electricity in 1951, the Coast Guard recommissioned it.

Heron Neck Light
NEAR VINALHAVEN
ESTABLISHED: 1854
Heron Neck Light actually stands on Green's Island near Vinalhaven. The original thirty-foot round granite lighthouse tower still stands, though it was automated in 1982. It's now leased by the Island Institute, a research and education institution.

Indian Island Light
ROCKPORT
ESTABLISHED: 1850
DEACTIVATED: 1934
The existing white square brick lighthouse here dates from 1874. It was deactivated in 1934 and replaced the next year by a pole. The property is now privately owned.

Isle Au Haut (Robinson Point) Light
ISLE AU HAUT
ESTABLISHED: 1907
Isle Au Haut Light is the last cylindrical brick lighthouse tower built in Maine; its design is similar to that of Marshall Point Light, connected to the keeper's quarters by a wooden walkway. Automated in 1934, the tower is owned by the town of Isle Au Haut, and the keeper's house is now a bed-and-breakfast inn. The lighthouse was renovated in 1999.

Libby Island Light

NEAR MACHIASPORT

ESTABLISHED: 1822

The original forty-two-foot granite Libby Island Light, which still stands, marks the entrance to Machias Bay. Automated in 1974, it's now part of a national wildlife refuge.

Little River Light

CUTLER

ESTABLISHED: 1847

DEACTIVATED: 1975

Little River Light overlooks Cutler Harbor, New England's northernmost protected harbor. The existing forty-one-foot brick-and-cast iron tower replaced the original in 1876. It was deactivated in 1975 and replaced by an automated light on a high pole. Now part of a bird sanctuary, the lighthouse has been leased to the American Lighthouse Foundation after being abandoned for twenty-five years.

Lubec Channel Light

LUBEC

ESTABLISHED: 1890

Another "spark plug"–style cast-iron lighthouse, the forty-foot Lubec Channel light was automated in 1939 and substantially renovated in 1993 to correct a pronounced tilt.

Wood End Light in Provincetown on Cape Cod

Marshall Point Light

ST. GEORGE

ESTABLISHED: 1832

The original tower built to mark the entrance to Port Clyde was succeeded in 1857 by the existing thirty-one-foot brick-and-granite structure; in 1895, the keeper's house was replaced after it was destroyed by lightning. Automated in 1980, the lighthouse is now owned by the town of St. George and houses the Marshall Point Lighthouse Museum; call 207-372-6450 for more information.

Matinicus Rock Light

NEAR MATINICUS ISLAND

ESTABLISHED: 1827

Along the approach to the Penobscot Bay, desolate Matinicus Rock was a prime spot for a lighthouse. The first twin towers, built in 1827, stood at opposite ends of a stone keeper's house. They were replaced in 1848 by a pair of granite towers, which were replaced again in 1857.

One of the two was extinguished along with most other twin lights in 1924; the other light was automated in 1983.

Monhegan Island Light

NEAR PORT CLYDE

ESTABLISHED: 1824

Thanks to the rough weather and high seas, the first granite lighthouse built on Monhegan Island soon had to be replaced with the existing forty-seven-foot tower, which went up in 1850. The keeper's house dates from 1874. All of the structures are now part of the Monhegan Museum, which houses an art collection and historical mementos. Automated in 1959, the light itself still operates. The museum is open during the summer and early fall; call 207-596-7003 for hours.

Moose Peak (Mistake Island) Light

NEAR JONESPORT

ESTABLISHED: 1827

Built in 1851 to guide ships safely across Eastern Bay, the existing fifty-seven-foot white brick lighthouse on this site was automated in 1972. Ten years later, a team of Green Berets blew up the keeper's house as a training exercise. The site is now leased to the Nature Conservancy.

Mount Desert Rock Light

NEAR FRENCHBORO

ESTABLISHED: 1830

Mount Desert Rock Light was built to mark a boulder more than twenty-five miles from shore at the entrance to Frenchman and Blue Hill Bays. The first lighthouse was a wooden tower beside a stone house. In 1847, the existing fifty-eight-foot granite tower was constructed. The light was automated in 1977.

Narraguagus (Pond Island) Light

NEAR MILBRIDGE

ESTABLISHED: 1853

DEACTIVATED: 1934

The original thirty-one-foot round granite tower still stands here, though it was taken out of service in 1934 and is now privately owned.

Nash Island Light

NEAR SOUTH ADDISON

ESTABLISHED: 1838

DEACTIVATED: 1982

At the southeast mouth of Pleasant Bay, Nash Island Light is a twenty-nine-foot square brick light with a tiny attached workroom. It was automated in 1958 and unceremoniously replaced by a buoy in 1982.

Owl's Head Light

OWL'S HEAD

ESTABLISHED: 1826

The original 1826 squat brick Owl's Head Light still stands, with its 1856 fourth-order Fresnel lens still in place, marking the entrance to Rockland Harbor. The lighthouse was automated in 1989. Today its keeper's quarters serves as Coast Guard housing, and the grounds are open to the public.

Pemaquid Point Light

NEAR BRISTOL

ESTABLISHED: 1827

With shipping—and shipwrecks—on the rise, a lighthouse marking the entrance to Muscongus Bay was built in 1827. The existing thirty-eight-foot stone tower was built in 1835, and the original fourth-order Fresnel lens installed in 1856 remains inside. Automated in 1934, the lighthouse now houses the Fisherman's Museum; call 207-677-2494 for more information.

Perkins Island Light

NEAR GEORGETOWN

ESTABLISHED: 1898

Another of the series of lighthouses strung along the Kennebec River in 1898, the twenty-three-foot Perkins Island Light was made of wood atop a brick foundation. It was automated in 1959, and remains in operation, guiding vessels to the river's mouth.

Petit Manan Light

NEAR MILLBRIDGE

ESTABLISHED: 1817

A stone tower was built here in 1817 to warn mariners of a shallow sandbar between the island of Petit Manan and Petit Manan Point. In 1855, the tower was replaced with the existing 119-foot granite lighthouse. The light was automated in 1972; today it is surrounded by the Petit Manan National Wildlife Refuge.

Pond Island Light

NEAR POPHAM BEACH

ESTABLISHED: 1821

On the rocky west side of the entrance to the Kennebec River, Pond Island Light stands near the first English settlement in the Northeast, the Popham Colony, which was established in 1607—a full thirteen years before the Pilgrims came ashore. American shipbuilding began at Popham Colony with the construction of the first ocean-going vessel ever built in North America, in which many of the Popham colonists hurriedly sailed home to England after experiencing their first Maine winter. The existing twenty-foot lighthouse tower dates from 1855; it was automated in 1963 and is now part of a bird refuge.

across the street from Salem's Customs House, and this squat brick lighthouse was built to mark it. The light was deactivated in 1977 and handed over to the National Park Service. It was relit with a solar-powered beacon as a private aid to navigation in 1983.

Duxbury Pier ("Bug") Light
DUXBURY
ESTABLISHED: 1871
A cast-iron lighthouse, Duxbury Pier Light marks a shoal beside the channel into Plymouth Harbor. Colloquially known as "Bug" Light, it was automated in 1964 and restored in 1984, thanks to local preservation efforts.

East Chop (Telegraph Hill) Light
OAK BLUFFS
ESTABLISHED: 1828
The first East Chop Light was privately built by a sea captain who received donations toward the cost from local merchants. The government took over in 1878 and built a new keeper's house and the existing squat cast-iron lighthouse, which was automated in 1933. The lighthouse is open to the public at times during the summer; call 508-627-4441 for more information.

Eastern Point Light
GLOUCESTER
ESTABLISHED: 1832
Eastern Point Light was built to help guide fishermen and others into Gloucester Harbor. The original thirty-foot stone lighthouse was replaced by a slightly taller model in 1848, and the existing structure was built in 1890. The lighthouse was automated in 1986 and restored by the Coast Guard in 1993.

Edgartown Harbor Light
EDGARTOWN
ESTABLISHED: 1828
Edgartown Harbor's first lighthouse sat just offshore on a stone pier connected to the mainland by a wooden causeway. Battered by the seas, the lighthouse and its causeway were finally destroyed by the hurricane of 1938. Rather than build a new lighthouse from scratch, the Coast Guard moved the abandoned 1873 cast-iron tower from Crane's Beach in Ipswich to the site. The Edgartown Harbor Light was automated in 1939. The

Sunrise on the granite cliffs below Bass Harbor Head Light in Maine's Acadia National Park

lighthouse is open by appointment; call 508-627-4441 for more information.

Fort Pickering (Winter Island) Light
SALEM
ESTABLISHED: 1871
DEACTIVATED: 1969
Named for the eighteenth-century fort that once stood here, Fort Pickering Light helped mark the route to Salem Harbor. It was built of cast iron and connected to the mainland by a wooden walkway. Deactivated in 1969, the lighthouse was abandoned and fell into disrepair until local volunteers refurbished it in 1983 and relit the beacon as a private aid to navigation.

Gay Head Light
GAY HEAD (AQUINNAH)
ESTABLISHED: 1799
The existing fifty-one-foot Gay Head Light was built in 1856, when it was ranked among the ten most important lighthouses, since it overlooked the aptly named ledge known as the Devil's Bridge. It became among the first in the country to receive a first-order Fresnel lens. Today the lighthouse is threatened by erosion, but the cliffs are slowly being stabilized. Visitors are allowed some evenings in the summer; call 508-627-4441 for more information.

Graves Light
BOSTON HARBOR
ESTABLISHED: 1905
One of the last offshore lighthouses built of stone instead of iron, Graves Light is a feat of engineering whose foundation alone took two years to construct. It was built just four feet above a ledge known as the Graves, astride a major shipping channel into Boston Harbor, with a lighthouse tower 113 feet above that. This lonely lighthouse remained staffed until 1976, when it was automated.

Great Point Light
NEAR NANTUCKET
ESTABLISHED: 1784
Also known as the Nantucket Lighthouse, Great Point replaced a beacon that was lit as early as 1769 at one tip of the island. The current seventy-foot tower is a modern-day (if slightly taller) replica of one built here in 1818, which was destroyed by a storm in 1984. The replacement was completed in 1986.

Highland (Cape Cod) Light
TRURO
ESTABLISHED: 1797
Highland Light marks the treacherous sandy outer Cape, and, to avoid being confused with Boston Light, was the first in the nation to display a flashing beacon. By 1996, the existing structure, which dated from 1857, stood barely 100 feet from the edge of a cliff. Volunteers raised more than $1.5 million to move it to safety. Visitors can now tour the lighthouse and the nearby Highland Museum; call 508-487-1121 for more information.

Hospital Point Light
BEVERLY
ESTABLISHED: 1872
Named for a smallpox hospital that once stood on the site, Hospital Point Light was built to help guide vessels into Beverly and Salem harbors. The Hospital Point Light is a front range lighthouse: Mariners take their bearings by triangulating it with the rear range light hidden in the steeple of the First Baptist Church. Though automated in 1947, the lighthouse still has its original third-and-a-half-order Fresnel lens; its keeper's house serves as the official quarters of the commander of the First U.S. Coast Guard District and his family.

Hyannis Range Rear Light
BARNSTABLE
ESTABLISHED: 1849
DEACTIVATED: 1929
This nineteen-foot brick tower helped vessels navigate narrow Hyannis Harbor. It was replaced when a breakwater was built in 1929 and is now part of a private home.

Long Island Head Light
BOSTON HARBOR
ESTABLISHED: 1820
DEACTIVATED: 1982 (REACTIVATED IN 1985)
Originally known as Inner Harbor Light, Long Island Head Light marks Boston Harbor's Long Island. Built on an eighty-six-foot hill on the island, it was originally only twenty-three feet tall. It was replaced in 1844 with an early prefabricated cast-iron lighthouse that was slightly higher, at thirty-four feet. The lighthouse was automated in 1918. It was briefly deactivated in the 1980s but has since been recommissioned.

Fort Pickering (Winter Island) Light in Salem, Massachusetts

museum in the keeper's house; call 401-466-5009 for more information.

Bristol Ferry Light

NEAR BRISTOL
ESTABLISHED: 1846
DEACTIVATED: 1927

A lightship marked the entrance to Bristol Harbor from 1846 until 1855, when ship captains petitioned the government for a proper lighthouse. They got a twenty-eight-foot tower attached to the front of a modest keeper's house, but the sixth-order Fresnel lens was visible for an impressive eleven miles. Deactivated in 1927, the lighthouse is now a private home whose owner has restored the lantern room and installed a purely decorative beacon.

Castle Hill Light

NEAR NEWPORT
ESTABLISHED: 1890

Marking Narragansett Bay's east passage, Castle Hill was a twenty-five-foot stone lighthouse on Castle Hill Cove. The keeper's house was destroyed in the hurricane of 1938; the light was automated in 1957.

Conanicut Island Light

NEAR JAMESTOWN
ESTABLISHED: 1886
DEACTIVATED: 1933

Built to help guide ships to busy Newport Harbor, Conanicut Island Light was a square wooden turret attached to a matching Gothic Revival–style keeper's quarters. It was replaced by a light on a pole in 1933, and now is privately owned, its lantern long ago removed.

Conimicut Shoal Light

NEAR WARWICK
ESTABLISHED: 1868

An offshore spark plug–style fifty-eight-foot cast-iron lighthouse built in 1883, Conimicut Shoal Light marks a hazard near the mouth of the Providence River. It was automated in 1966.

Dutch Island Light

NEAR JAMESTOWN
ESTABLISHED: 1826
DEACTIVATED: 1979

Modeled on Beavertail Light, Dutch Island Light sits atop a square brick forty-two-foot tower. It is now part of a state park, maintained under lease to the American Lighthouse Foundation.

Hog Island Shoal Light

NEAR PORTSMOUTH
ESTABLISHED: 1886

An offshore cast-iron lighthouse on a granite base, Hog Island Shoal Light replaced a lightship marking the shoal at the entrance to Bristol Harbor. Now automated, it was renovated by the Coast Guard in 1995.

Ida Lewis Rock (Lime Rock) Light

NEWPORT
ESTABLISHED: 1854
DEACTIVATED: 1927

Originally a short stone tower to which the keeper had to row each night, Lime Rock Light quickly got a connecting keeper's house in 1856. There the famous keeper Ida Lewis spent thirty-five years, rescuing dozens of people and entertaining presidents and millionaires. When she died in 1901, the lighthouse was renamed in her honor. Now the headquarters of the Ida Lewis Yacht Club and a private aid to navigation, it continues to shine its modern electric beacon every night from Memorial Day to Columbus Day.

Nayatt Point Light

NEAR BARRINGTON
ESTABLISHED: 1828
DEACTIVATED: 1868

Built to mark the mouth of the Providence River, this twenty-five-foot square brick tower was used for only forty years, and its fourth-order Fresnel lens was moved to Conimicut Shoal Light. It is now privately owned.

Newport Harbor (Goat Island) Light

NEWPORT
ESTABLISHED: 1824

Newport boasted one of America's busiest harbors in the seventeenth and eighteenth centuries, and by 1824, its entrance had been marked with a lighthouse at the northern tip of Goat Island. But the light was dim, and the location was inadequate, so the original light was moved to Prudence Island (where it still stands) and replaced by the existing tower, which has since been automated. The keeper's house, built in 1865, was torn down after being hit in 1922 by a submarine on a test cruise.

Boston Light, America's oldest lighthouse station

Plum Beach Light

NEAR NORTH KINGSTOWN

ESTABLISHED: 1897

DEACTIVATED: 1941

This cast-iron lighthouse on a concrete pier marks the west passage of Narragansett Bay. The lighthouse was severely damaged by the hurricane of 1938. Three years later, with the construction of the Jamestown Bridge, Plum Beach Light was deactivated. Tied up for years by litigation over, among other things, the question of who owned it, the lighthouse is now in the hands of a non-profit organization, which is raising money to restore it.

Point Judith Light

POINT JUDITH

ESTABLISHED: 1810

Point Judith Light was preceded by a day marker as early as the early 1700s. The first lighthouse was destroyed by a hurricane in 1815. The next tower was badly built and soon in disrepair, and sixteen vessels were wrecked nearby in 1855 alone. The existing lighthouse was constructed two years later, and a lifesaving station was added in 1872. While the lifesaving station and the keeper's house have been torn down, the original 1857 fourth-order Fresnel lens remains in operation in the tower, which is now

Derby Wharf Light in Salem Harbor, Massachusetts

part of a Coast Guard station. The grounds are open to the public.

Pomham Rocks Light

EAST PROVIDENCE
ESTABLISHED: 1871
DEACTIVATED: 1974

A predecessor to, and close cousin of, New London Ledge Light in Connecticut, Pomham Rocks Light consists of a lantern on top of a wooden French Second Empire house. Unlike the offshore New London Ledge Light, however, Pomham Rocks sits on a bluff along the Providence River. Replaced in 1974 by a light on a tall pole, the keeper's house and tower are now privately owned; the fourth-order Fresnel lens is in the Custom House Maritime Museum in Newburyport, Massachusetts.

Poplar Point Light

NEAR NORTH KINGSTOWN
ESTABLISHED: 1831
DEACTIVATED: 1882

Poplar Point Light marks Wickford Harbor. It was replaced by Wickford Harbor Light, and, with its handsome Cape Cod–style keeper's house, is now privately owned.

Prudence Island (Sandy Point) Light

PRUDENCE ISLAND
ESTABLISHED: 1852

Prudence Island Light was moved here from Goat Island in Newport Harbor in 1851 to mark the passage between Prudence Island and the mainland. The

keeper's house was destroyed in the hurricane of 1938, killing the keeper's wife and son and three other people. The keeper, George Gustavus, survived, but never went back to the lighthouse. Prudence Island Light was automated in 1961.

Rose Island Light

NEWPORT
ESTABLISHED: 1870
DEACTIVATED: 1971

This sturdy lighthouse was made obsolete with the construction of the Newport Bridge in 1969 and decommissioned in 1971. Volunteer preservationists have since restored it, and it is now used as a guest house and museum, with the beacon, now privately maintained, shining from the lantern room. The museum is open during the summer; call 401-847-4242 for more information.

Sakonnet Point Light

NEAR SAKONNET
ESTABLISHED: 1884
DEACTIVATED: 1955 (REACTIVATED IN 1997)

A cast-iron tower on a concrete pier about 800 yards offshore, Sakonnet Point Light was damaged by the hurricanes of 1938 and 1954, when it was decommissioned and abandoned. Since repaired by volunteers, it was recommissioned by an act of Congress and relit in 1997.

Warwick Light

WARWICK
ESTABLISHED: 1827

Warwick Light marks Warwick Neck, a navigational hazard in Narragansett Bay. The existing fifty-one-foot cast-iron tower was one of the last built in New England; it went up in 1932. Only seven years later, it had to be moved away from the eroding shoreline. In 1985, the lighthouse also became one of the last to be automated.

Watch Hill Light

WATCH HILL
ESTABLISHED: 1808

Watch Hill had a rudimentary beacon marking the eastern entrance to Fishers Island Sound as early as 1745. A wooden lighthouse was built in 1808, making it the second in Rhode Island. Threatened with erosion in 1856, it was replaced with a forty-five-foot square granite tower. A lifesaving station was added in the 1870s. Watch Hill Light was automated in 1986. The oil house now serves as a museum; call 401-789-4422 for more information.

Connecticut

Avery Point Light
GROTON
ESTABLISHED: 1943
DEACTIVATED: 1967
The last lighthouse built in Connecticut, Avery Point served as both a navigational aid and a ceremonial tower on the grounds of what was then a U.S. Coast Guard training station.

Black Rock Harbor (Fayerweather Island) Light
BRIDGEPORT
ESTABLISHED: 1808
DEACTIVATED: 1932
A lighthouse on Fayerweather Island has marked the entrance to Black Rock Harbor since 1808, when a forty-foot tower was built. Destroyed in a hurricane, it was replaced in 1823 with the existing light. In 1932, the lighthouse was replaced with an offshore beacon. Badly damaged by neglect and vandalism, it was restored in 1983 and again in 1998. The grounds are open to the public.

Bridgeport Breakwater (Tongue Point) Light
BRIDGEPORT
ESTABLISHED: 1895
Built on a pier on one side of the harbor, the thirty-one-foot black cast-iron tower was moved to its current location in 1919.

Faulkners Island Light
GUILFORD
ESTABLISHED: 1802
Faulkners Island's rocky shallows claimed countless vessels navigating Long Island Sound until a lighthouse could be built here. The 1871 keeper's house was destroyed by a fire in 1976, and the tower was vandalized. But the biggest threat has been erosion. A 1999 renovation of the lighthouse—the second-oldest in Connecticut—included building a stone revetment around three-quarters of the island, which is now a bird sanctuary.

Five Mile Point Light
NEW HAVEN
ESTABLISHED: 1805
DEACTIVATED: 1877
The original Five Mile Point Light, marking the entrance to New Haven Harbor, was quickly considered inad-equate and, after endless bureaucratic delays, was finally replaced in 1847 by the current sandstone tower, with a fourth-order Fresnel lens added eight years later. It was deactivated on January 1, 1877, when the light at nearby Southwest Ledge went into operation. With the exterior restored in 1986, Five Mile Point Light is now the centerpiece of New Haven's Lighthouse Point Park.

Great Captain Island Light
near GREENWICH
ESTABLISHED: 1829
DEACTIVATED: 1970
The first lighthouse on Great Captain Island was built of stone in 1829, but it was badly constructed and poorly equipped. Although a fourth-order Fresnel lens was installed in 1858, the tower needed to be replaced by 1868. The new structure, made of granite, used the same design as its counterparts at Block Island North and Sheffield Island, among others. It was deactivated in 1970 and replaced by a light on a forty-foot steel tower. Local businesses have helped renovate the lighthouse.

Greens Ledge Light
near NORWALK
ESTABLISHED: 1902
This cast-iron offshore lighthouse marks a mile-long ledge that confounded vessels making their way to Norwalk Harbor. Still in operation, the lighthouse was automated in 1972.

Latimer Reef Light
near MYSTIC
ESTABLISHED: 1804
The oldest active cast-iron lighthouse in the Northeast, the current Latimer Reef Light was built in 1884 to replace a bare iron spire that was often carried away by ice; before that, a private lightship was moored at the site. It marks a rocky shoal one mile north of East Point on Fishers Island, near the entrance to Stonington Harbor. The three-story brick-lined iron tower has living quarters on three levels and the watch deck on the fourth.

Lynde Point (Saybrook) Light
OLD SAYBROOK
ESTABLISHED: 1803
Lynde Point Light marks the entrance to the Connecticut River and Old Saybrook Harbor. Its first incarnation proved too short, so a higher granite tower was constructed in 1838 and a fourth-order Fresnel lens installed

Black Rock Harbor (Fayerweather Island) Light in Connecticut

in 1858, the same year that a wood-frame keeper's house was built. The fourth-order lens was replaced by a fifth-order lens in 1890. The keeper's house was torn down in 1966, but the tower, with its 1890 Fresnel lens, was automated in 1978 and remains active.

Morgan Point Light
NOANK
ESTABLISHED: 1831
DEACTIVATED: 1919
A twenty-five-foot granite tower was built here in 1831 to guide ships to the entrance of the Mystic River and Noank Harbor. The beacon was brightened by a sixth-order Fresnel lens in 1855, but by 1867 a new lighthouse was needed. The next year a granite house was built with a lantern tower attached at the front like a church steeple. Replaced by a light on a steel tower in 1919, it was sold and is now a private home.

New London Harbor Light
NEW LONDON
ESTABLISHED: 1760
A beacon existed at the entrance to New London Harbor since 1750, replaced in 1760 by a sixty-four-foot stone tower. It was the fourth lighthouse in North America and the first on Long Island Sound. In 1801, the existing eighty-nine-foot light was built. It remains the oldest lighthouse in Connecticut. The lighthouse has been automated since 1912; the keeper's house, which was built in 1863, is now a private home.

New London Ledge Light
NEW LONDON
ESTABLISHED: 1909
One of the oldest lighthouses in New England, New London Ledge Light looks as if it is floating in the entrance to New London Harbor, where it sits atop a fifty-two-foot-square concrete foundation and marks a 200-foot-long shoal. The last staffed lighthouse on Long Island Sound, it was automated in 1987. Today it uses solar power.

Pecks Ledge Light
NEAR NORWALK
ESTABLISHED: 1906
An offshore cast-iron lighthouse shaped like a spark plug, Pecks Ledge Light marks a ledge at the east end of the Norwalk Islands near the opening to Norwalk Harbor. It was automated in 1933.

Penfield Reef Light
NEAR FAIRFIELD
ESTABLISHED: 1874
One of the most dangerous places on Long Island Sound, Penfield Reef had claimed enough lives and valuable shipping by 1874 to merit the construction of this expensive offshore granite lighthouse, which was among the last to be built before the government switched to cheaper cast-iron designs. It is reported to be haunted by the ghost of Fred Jordan, a keeper who drowned while rowing ashore for Christmas leave in 1916. The light was automated in 1971.

Saybrook Breakwater Light
OLD SAYBROOK
ESTABLISHED: 1886
Located on the westernmost of two stone jetties built to protect Old Saybrook Harbor from being clogged with

shifting sand, this cast-iron lighthouse helped guide ships into the dredged deep channel. It was automated in 1959, and the exterior was restored by the Coast Guard in 1996.

Sheffield Island (Norwalk) Light

NEAR NORWALK

ESTABLISHED: 1828

DEACTIVATED: 1902

Sheffield Island Light was built to warn against a dangerous ledge at the mouth of Norwalk Harbor. As the island's shore eroded, the lighthouse had to be replaced in 1868; the remains of the original now lie underwater. The existing Sheffield Island Light, made of granite, was replaced in 1902 by Greens Ledge Light and consequently was sold. Today the lighthouse is owned by the Norwalk Seaport Association, which offers visits by passenger ferry weekends in the summer; call 203-838-9444 for more information.

Southwest Ledge (New Haven Breakwater) Light

NEW HAVEN

ESTABLISHED: 1877

Southwest Ledge Light was one of the first to be built on a circular offshore iron foundation, considered so revolutionary that a copy of it was displayed at the 1876 Centennial Exposition. It replaced Five Mile Point Light and marked an underwater rock formation astride the main route to New Haven Harbor. Despite its much-heralded design, the octagonal cast-iron lighthouse was plagued by cracks in the base, leaks, and insect infestations. It was automated in 1973.

Stamford Harbor (Chatham Rocks) Light

STAMFORD

ESTABLISHED: 1882

DEACTIVATED: 1953

A seven-story prefabricated cast-iron tower on an offshore cylindrical pier, Stamford Harbor marked the treacherous Chatham Rocks reef at the entrance to Stamford Harbor. Deactivated in 1953, it was sold to a succession of owners, including one who restored it as a private home but never lived there.

Stonington Harbor Light

STONINGTON

ESTABLISHED: 1823

DEACTIVATED: 1889

Built in 1823 on Stonington Point, the first Stonington Harbor Light had to soon be replaced due to erosion. A new lighthouse was built on the east side of the harbor in 1840, using some of the stone from the original lighthouse. The new light was deactivated in 1889 with the construction of the cast-iron Stonington Breakwater Light; a hurricane destroyed the breakwater light in 1938. The 1840 lighthouse was purchased by the town's historical society and has been a museum since 1925; call 860-535-1440 for more information.

Stratford Point Light

STRATFORD

ESTABLISHED: 1822

The mouth of the Housatonic River and Stratford Harbor had been marked by a bonfire and then by a fire in an iron basket on a pole before a lighthouse finally was built. In 1881, it was replaced with a thirty-five-foot cast-iron tower with a third-order Fresnel lens and a keeper's house. Coast Guard personnel now live in the keeper's quarters; the grounds are open to the public.

Stratford Shoal (Middle Ground) Light

BRIDGEPORT

ESTABLISHED: 1877

The reefs of Stratford Shoal in busy Long Island Sound were marked by a succession of fixed buoys and a lightship before construction of a lighthouse finally began there in 1874. Stratford Shoal Light's foundation alone took more than two years and tons of stone to build. The difficulty and cost made this one of the last such masonry towers built offshore before the government turned to less expensive cast-iron-and-concrete designs. Automated in 1970, the light remains in use.

New York (Long Island)

Cedar Island Light

SAG HARBOR

ESTABLISHED: 1839

DEACTIVATED: 1934

Built to guide whaling ships into Long Island's Port of Sag Harbor, Cedar Island Light was originally a thirty-five-foot wooden tower. It was replaced in 1868 with the present granite lighthouse. The hurricane of 1938 filled in the 200-yard strait that once separated the property from the mainland and converted the island into a peninsula. By then, however, the light had been moved to a skeleton tower and the lighthouse deactivated.

Portland Head Light in Cape Elizabeth, Maine

Cold Spring Harbor Light

CENTER ISLAND

ESTABLISHED: 1890

DEACTIVATED: 1965

Originally on Point of Shoal, this square wooden tower was removed from its concrete-filled cast-iron foundation and moved to a private estate as a decoration.

Eatons Neck Light

EATONS NECK

ESTABLISHED: 1799

On a high bluff overlooking Long Island Sound, Eatons Neck is the second-oldest lighthouse on Long Island. In 1849, Eatons Neck also became the site of the first life-saving station built by the federal government; it is still used as housing for U.S. Coast Guard personnel. The third-order Fresnel lens installed in 1858 remains, though it is now powered by a 1,000-watt quartz filament bulb instead of whale oil lamps.

Execution Rocks Light

NEAR SANDS POINT

ESTABLISHED: 1850

Signaling the approach to New York City from the northeast, Execution Rocks Light shines its original fourth-order Fresnel lens from an artificial island made of boulders in thirty-seven feet of water off Sands Point. The forty-two-foot granite tower stands on a site used by British colonial officials to execute political prisoners. Before the addition of the attached granite house in 1867, keepers and their wives lived in the tower.

Fire Island Light

SALTAIRE

ESTABLISHED: 1827

DEACTIVATED: 1974 (REACTIVATED IN 1986)

Mariners complained that the first Fire Island Light, built in 1827 to mark the eastern entrance to New York Harbor, was too short to be seen at sea. The outcry reached its climax in 1850, when a ship broke up and sank almost within sight of the lighthouse. The current 180-foot lighthouse was completed in 1858. A critical light for transatlantic steamers bound for New York, Fire Island got a first-order Fresnel lens. Deactivated in 1974, the structure was rescued by the Fire Island Lighthouse Preservation Society and reactivated in 1986. There is a museum inside; call 631-321-7028 for more information.

Horton Point Light

NEAR SOUTHOLD

ESTABLISHED: 1790

DEACTIVATED: 1933 (REACTIVATED IN 1990)

Horton Point Light shines from a cliff 103 feet above high tide along a stretch of coast once known as Dead Man's Cove, on the northeastern shore of Long Island. Decommissioned in 1933, it was briefly revived as a lookout for enemy aircraft during World War II and was reactivated on its bicentennial in 1990. Today it also houses the Southold, New York, Historical Society Nautical Museum; call 631-321-7028 for more information.

Huntington Harbor Light

HUNTINGTON VILLAGE

ESTABLISHED: 1857

A square tower attached to a one-story dwelling on a round concrete foundation, Huntington Harbor Light is the oldest reinforced concrete lighthouse on the East Coast. It was nicknamed the Castle, but conditions were far from royal; the first keepers reached the lantern by climbing a ladder to a second-story window, often during rain or snow.

Little Gull Island Light

NEAR ORIENT POINT

ESTABLISHED: 1806

An eighty-one-foot granite tower on a granite pier, this current tower dates from 1869 and stands off Fishers Island. Although the light remains in use, the keeper's quarters was dismantled in 1978. The original second-order Fresnel lens is in the East End Seaport Museum in Greenport.

Montauk Point Light

NEAR MONTAUK

ESTABLISHED: 1796

Montauk Point was for years the first landmark to greet arriving immigrants, giving it great symbolic value. Commissioned by George Washington, it has walls seven feet thick at the base and a foundation thirteen feet deep. Although this sturdy workmanship has stood the test of time, erosion has threatened the seventy-eight-foot sandstone tower; the shore has moved from 300 feet to within fifty-seven feet of the lighthouse in the last 200 years. The third-and-one-half-order Fresnel lens used here until 1987 is displayed in the former keeper's quarters. For more information, call 631-668-2544.

North Dumpling Light

FISHERS ISLAND

ESTABLISHED: 1849

DEACTIVATED: 1959 (REACTIVATED: 1980)

The mansard-roofed combination red brick keeper's house and tower now on this site was built in 1871 and deactivated in 1959 in favor of an automated light atop a pole. The house was sold to private owners, and in an unusual arrangement, the light was later restored to the top of their roof.

Old Field Point Light

OLD FIELD

ESTABLISHED: 1823

DEACTIVATED: 1933 (REACTIVATED: 1991)

Thousands of coastal freighters, passenger vessels, and mail ships crowded Long Island Sound in the pre-rail-road days, when Old Field Point Light was built in 1823. Its successor, built in 1868, is a sturdy granite house with a seventy-four-foot lantern tower. The 1823 keeper's dwelling now serves as the Old Field village hall; the second floor of the 1868 lighthouse, which is still active, is the residence of the village's first constable. The grounds are open to the public by appointment; call 631-941-9412 for more information.

Orient Point Light

ORIENT POINT

ESTABLISHED: 1899

One of the first no-frills cast-iron lighthouses, Orient Point was made of overlapping prefabricated boiler plates on a cast-iron foundation weighted with concrete. The light marks Oyster Pond Reef, a ledge just beneath the surface of Plum Gut; an earlier beacon there was swept away by ice in 1896. Rust holes and cracks in the foundation have gradually created a five-degree tilt, but the lighthouse, nicknamed Old Coffee Pot, remains active.

Plum Island (Plum Gut) Light

NEAR ORIENT

ESTABLISHED: 1827

DEACTIVATED: 1978

Along with Orient Point Light, Plum Island Light marked the fast-streaming waters of Plum Gut, used by vessels passing up and down Long Island Sound. The light stands on an island a mile and a half from the northeastern end of Long Island and is named for the beach plums that grow there. The government replaced it with an automated light in 1978. Its only neighbor is the U.S. Department of Agriculture, which quarantines and studies diseased animals on the island.

Race Rock Light

FISHERS ISLAND

ESTABLISHED: 1879

Race Rock Light marks a ledge barely exposed at low tide in a passage that claimed eight vessels between 1829 and 1837 alone. Buoys and beacons fixed to the ledge were quickly swept away. An engineering feat thought to be impossible, the construction of the lighthouse required thousands of tons of boulders to be brought in to stabilize the sixty-nine-foot circular foundation; the light took more than seven years to build, with masons sometimes working underwater. Despite the success of the project, its cost and difficulty led the Lighthouse Board to develop the cast-iron caisson lighthouse.

Sands Point Light

SANDS POINT

ESTABLISHED: 1809

DEACTIVATED: 1922

Sands Point Light was built by a sea captain, Noah Mason, on land he owned; he then served as its first keeper. A brick colonial was attached in 1868. In 1917, the adjacent property became the estate of Mrs. Oliver Hazard Perry Belmont, whose first husband was William K. Vanderbilt, one of the wealthiest men in America, and the parties she held there are said to have inspired F. Scott Fitzgerald's The Great Gatsby. In 1922, the lighthouse was replaced by a beacon on a steel tower 325 feet offshore at the outer edge of a reef.

Stepping Stones Light

NEAR KINGS POINT

ESTABLISHED: 1877

This mansard-roofed red brick house and lantern tower stand 1,600 yards off Long Island, guarding the approach to the East River. The light was supposed to be built on Hart Island, but the government couldn't reach agreement with the owner, so an offshore foundation was provided using 900 tons of boulders piled on a rock that barely broke the surface at low tide. The lighthouse still has its original 1889 Fresnel lens.

Maine's Cape Neddick ("the Nubble") Light silhouetted by a sunrise

Bibliography

Clayton, Barbara, and Kathleen Whitley. *Exploring Coastal Massachusetts: New Bedford to Salem*. New York: Dodd, Mead, 1983.

Clifford, Candace. *1994 Inventory of Historic Light Stations*. Washington, D.C.: National Maritime Initiative, National Park Service, 1994.

Clifford, Mary Louise, and J. Candace Clifford. *Women Who Kept the Lights: An Illustrated History of Female Lighthouse Keepers*. Williamsburg, Va.: Cypress Communications, 1993.

De Wire, Elinor. *Guardians of the Lights: Stories of U.S. Lighthouse Keepers*. Sarasota, Fla.: Pineapple Press, 1995.

Feller-Roth, Barbara. *Lighthouses: A Guide to Coastal and Offshore Guardians*. Freeport, Maine: DeLorme Publishing Co., 1983.

Grant, John, and Ray Jones. *Legendary Lighthouses*. Old Saybrook, Conn.: Globe Pequot Press, 1998.

Hamilton, Harlan. *Lights and Legends: An Historical Guide to Lighthouses of Long Island Sound, Fisher's Island Sound, and Block Island Sound*. Stamford, Conn.: Wescott Cove Publishing Co., 1987.

Holland, F. Ross, Jr. *Great American Lighthouses*. New York: John Wiley & Sons, 1994.

Kochel, Kenneth G. *America's Atlantic Coast Lighthouses*. Clearwater, Fla.: Kenneth Kochel Publishing, 1998.

Noble, Dennis. *Lighthouses and Keepers: The U.S. Lighthouse Service and Its Legacy*. Annapolis, Md.: Naval Institute Press, 1997.

Nordhoff, Charles. *The Lighthouses of the United States in 1874*. Silverthorne, Colo.: Vistabooks Publishing, 1992.

Roberts, Bruce, and Ray Jones. *Northern Lighthouses: New Brunswick to the Jersey Shore*. Old Saybrook, Conn.: Globe Pequot Press, 1994.

Roberts, Kenneth Lewis. *Boon Island, Including Contemporary Accounts of the Wreck of the Nottingham Galley*. ed. Jack Bales and Richard Warner. Hanover, N.H.: University Press of New England, 1996.

Snow, Edward Rowe. *Adventures, Blizzards, and Coastal Calamities*. New York: Dodd, Mead, 1978.

Snow, Edward Rowe. *Boston Bay Mysteries and Other Tales*. New York: Dodd, Mead, 1977.

Snow, Edward Rowe. *Great Storms and Famous Shipwrecks of the New England Coast*. Boston: Yankee Publishing Co., 1944.

Snow, Edward Rowe. *The Lighthouses of New England, 1716–1973*. New York: Dodd, Mead, 1973.

Sterling, Robert T. *Lighthouses of the Maine Coast and the Men Who Keep Them*. Brattleboro, Vt.: Stephen Daye Press, 1935.

And on the Web:

American Lighthouse Foundation: www.lighthousefoundation.org
Legendary Lighthouses: www.pbs.org/legendarylighthouses/
Lighthouse Preservation Society: www.maine.com/lights/lps.htm
Lighthouses, Lightships, and Aids to Navigation (U.S. Coast Guard): www.uscg.mil/hq/g-cp/history/h_lhindex.htm
National Marine Initiative (National Park Service): www.cr.nps.gov/maritime/lt_index.htm
New England Lighthouses: A Virtual Guide: www.lighthouse.cc/
United States Lighthouse Society: www.maine.com/lights/uslhs.htm

Index

About the Author and Photographer

Photograph by Julie Quinlivan

Photograph by Gary M. Blazon

A lifelong New Englander, author Jon Marcus is executive editor at *Boston Magazine*. He also has contributed to *Yankee, New England Travel & Life, Conde Nast Traveler*, and other magazines, and to the *Boston Globe, Chicago Tribune, Los Angeles Times, Miami Herald, Newsday, Washington Post*, and other newspapers; and is a U.S. education correspondent for *The Times of London*.

Marcus is the author of *Unknown New England* and *Boston: A CityLife Pictorial Guide* (Voyageur Press, 1998).

A graduate of Bates College and the Graduate School of Journalism at Columbia University, Marcus also attended Oxford University.

———○———

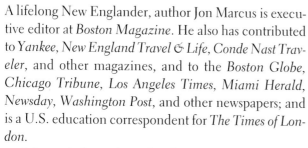

Photographer Susan Cole Kelly specializes in capturing the beauty of the American landscape with the intimate details of people and places. A New England native, she majored in art at the University of New Hampshire, studied photography at the New England School of Photography, and took master classes at the Maine Photographic Workshops.

Kelly previously teamed up with author Jon Marcus to produce the book *Boston: A CityLife Pictorial Guide* (Voyageur Press, 1998). She also has contributed to the *Audubon Guide to New England, National Geographic Society Guide to Birdwatching*, and *Boston – History in the Making*.

A regular contributor to *New England Travel & Life*, the American Park Network guides to national parks, and the *Alaskan Milepost*, Kelly also has illustrated articles for *Vermont Life, Downeast, Yankee, Touring America*, and *Historic Traveler* magazines. Her photographs have been featured in wall calendars, postcards, and engagement calendars, including an exclusive Boston calendar published annually by Browntrout Publishers.

Susan Cole Kelly is a member of the American Society of Media Photographers and makes her home in Boston's historic North End.